MADE IN MANITOBA

BEST
OF THE
OPEN
ROAD
STORIES

Copyright 2011 © Bill Redekop

Published by
MacIntyre Purcell Publishing Inc.
232 Lincoln St., PO Box 1142
Lunenburg, Nova Scotia
B0J 2C0 Canada
www.macintyrepurcell.com

www.facebook.com/madeinmanitoba
www.twitter.com/madeinmanitoba

We acknowledge the support of the Department of Canadian Heritage and the Nova Scotia Department of Communities, Culture and Heritage in the development of writing and publishing in Canada.

Printed and bound in Canada by Friesens.

Library and Archives Canada Cataloguing in Publication
Redekop, Bill
      Made in Manitoba : best of the
Open road stories / Bill Redekop.

Stories originally published in the Winnipeg Free Press.
ISBN 978-1-926916-11-8

      1. Manitoba--Social life and customs--Anecdotes.
2. Manitoba--Rural conditions--Anecdotes. 3. Country
life--Manitoba--Anecdotes. I. Title.

FC3368.R43 2011   971.27   C2011-903959-1

If you have any rural story ideas, please pass them along to **bill.redekop@freepress.mb.ca**

Photo Credits
Cover: istockphoto; Mike Aporius: page 142, 144, 172; Associated Press: page 203; Ruth Bonneville: page 139; Brandon Sun archives: page 74; Joe Bryksa: page 40, 47, 62, 71, 196, 197; Bruce Bumstead: page 53, 67; Colin Corneau: page 14, 158, 166; Jeff De Booy: page 126, 137, 202; Hal G. Duncan, *The South-West Corner*: page 119, 124; Joe Gabski: page 114, 115; Marc Gallant: page 111; Ken Gigliotti: page 27, 28, 42, 45, 61, 204, 210, 214-16, 222; Wayne Glowacki: page 12, 21, 22, 96, 163, 179, 188; Fred Greenslade: page 54, 57, 105; Trevor Hagan: page 86; Mary Herd: page 127, 219; Phil Hossack: page 102, 180, 192, 195; *Looking Back: A History of Mountain Road*: page 43; Boris Minkevich: page 145; NBC photo: page 93; Bill Redekop: page 17, 24, 31, 34, 113, 116, 121, 131, 135, 199; Tim Smith: page 83; Tom Thomson: page 207; University of Manitoba Archives — Grove Collection: page 33.

MADE IN MANITOBA

BEST
OF THE
OPEN
ROAD
STORIES

Bill Redekop

Contents

For Ike and Marge Redekop

Introduction

Ten years of travelling the province writing stories for the *Winnipeg Free Press*. I can hardly believe it.

I didn't set out to be this rambling rural reporter for the paper.

I'm one of those people for whom other people always seem to know what's best. I didn't apply to be a reporter with the *Free Press*. I was quite content where I was at the farm weekly, *Manitoba Co-operator*. Then *Free Press* city editor Pat Flynn phoned me one day and, as is his wont, pretty much got around to the reason for the call within the first 15 seconds. "We'd like you to come work for us," he said.

I didn't come up with the idea to write true crime books, either. Great Plains Publications owner Gregg Shilliday approached me. I wasn't a crime reporter at all. "I'd like you to write a book about some of Manitoba's most famous crimes and criminals," Shilliday said. Really? Me? The result was *Crimes of the Century*, and *Crime Stories*, both now out of print, unfortunately.

I was less eager when approached to take on the post of rural reporter for the *Free Press*. I turned the job down twice. The offers came about two years apart. I turned the job down for two main reasons. One was it wasn't important enough. I wanted to do more important work at the newspaper, one of the glory jobs. Maybe somewhere down the line I could be rural reporter.

The other reason I refused is because the two previous rural reporters had quit abruptly and they had quit, by and large, because of interference from editors. It's not that the editors were evil; it's just that editors never have enough resources to cover news, as opposed to the less time-sensitive stories a rural reporter writes. They just can't keep their hands off a reporter who isn't writing for tomorrow's paper. My two predecessors were testament to that.

So I said no. I was emphatic about that.

Finally, our managing editor at the time, Nicholas Hirst, got involved. I'm sure Nick was behind the solicitations all along. He told me he thought I would be perfect for the post and wanted to know why I wouldn't do it. I didn't get into the first reason but I did tell him the second reason. The newspaper didn't treat rural coverage like a real beat. If it wasn't a real beat, I wasn't interested.

I'm thankful to Nick today, just as I'm thankful to all the other people who knew what was best for me when I didn't. He set it up in such a way that gave the rural reporter independence and freedom to roam this province. If he saw me in the office, he'd try to kick me out. "What are you doing in here? Get out, get out," he'd say.

Margo Goodhand, the current managing editor, came along later and moved me up from the back pages. Margo both gave me a forum, called Open Road, and freedom to write longer features.

The result has been unique coverage in Canada. I don't know of another daily newspaper that has a dedicated rural reporter. I know it's tried from time to time but I've never seen it work for very long. One editor told me when I started that I wouldn't still be doing the beat after two years. His thinking, I believe, was that there wasn't enough material to sustain such a beat.

So for these reasons, that my position put me in conflict with editors immediately above me, that many newspaper apparatchiks don't believe there is content for such a beat, and also because I have a distrusting nature, I've always felt my position was tenuous. I've always felt like Scheherazade.

Scheherazade is the wife of Persian King Shahryar, who staves off her execution each night by diverting him with a story. Betrayed by his first wife, the freakishly powerful king has concluded he must kill his new brides after each wedding night to be on the safe side. So Scheherazade spins these wonderful yarns each night to take the king's mind off his misogyny. Hence, *One Thousand and One Arabian Nights*.

There aren't 1,001 stories here, thank goodness, but I have always felt the sword of King Shahryar hovering, compelling me to come up with interesting stories. If not for the threat, I would be back chained to my office desk. Which would almost feel like death now.

Ah, the country. Take a deep breath. What an incredible landscape to put to canvas.

It's a bit like the slow food movement, in terms of news gathering. Instead of doing the stories by 15-minute telephone interview, you drive up all these long narrow driveways. Dogs come running out to see who you are. Only occasionally have I decided I'd better stay in the car until someone came out. My funniest farm-dog story involves a chihuahua. It's true. I stayed in the car and looked around. Well, this seems safe, I said to myself. I was expecting a pack of wild dogs to come running up behind that yappy little hairless chihuahua, but it was the only farm dog. It was like that old Superbowl commercial about the cat herders. "Herdin' cats. Don't let anyone tell you it's easy," a cowboy says.

I've seen wolves, coyotes, snapping turtles, deer, while on assignment. I've driven along gravel farm roads, in August, with naked farm fields all around and high, lush grasses growing right up to the shoulder, and had a deer jump out of the grassy ditch as if out of thin air and almost hit me. I've stripped down to my shorts on an empty farm road after a short walk through some grasses to look at the Souris River, only to find myself covered with wood ticks. I pulled off something like 35 and, believe me, those ticks can move when they want to. They were just running up my legs.

The slow-motion, collapsing trapezoid farm buildings, the rusted vintage car on the edge of a field, the family photos on the fridge door, all become part of the story somehow. So do the busy café at coffee time, the "Be Back Soon" signs in shop windows, the rubber tire from a tree overhanging a little river, the coiling, caramel-coloured flypaper hanging from the ceiling with its catch for all to see. Every naked light bulb shining above a community hall entrance, every moon-like yard light glowing in the distance, feel like parts of the tales I've written. I've stayed in many bed-and-breakfasts and gone for solitary walks down their gravel connections in the evening. I've come to know hotel owners by their first names, and rely on them for local information the way newspaper columnist Alan Fotheringham used to rely on cab drivers.

I happened to read the other day, in the midst of composing this introduction, an essay in the *London Review of Books* by August Kleinzahler about road stories.

"The literature of car trips across America usually revolves around colourful local characters the narrator meets along the way. This is true of [John] Steinbeck, [Jack] Kerouac, William Least Heat-Moon in his Blue Highways and so on."

It's true that it's the people you meet along the way who make the road trip. But I wouldn't say it takes colourful characters, or even characters. I've certainly met colourful characters — you couldn't get more colourful, or more enjoyable, than Henry Makinson and his dancing bison. But I find a lot of people are pretty colourful on the inside in less obvious ways. I tend to be at least as interested in a rich inner life as a rich outer one.

It's hard to say which are the most memorable stories. Things memorable to me might not be for readers. One story I've always liked is Dennis Dunlop's business just outside Ste. Anne. Dunlop made cedar shims. Just shims. Nothing else. It reminded me so much of helping my dad. My dad built a lot of things and he was always shimming. We'd have to shim a floor board or a window, make a shim out of something to level something or other, or use a shim to stir the paint or contact cement or whatever. To be honest, I was bored by a lot of it and hardly even knew what my dad was talking about with his shims. But we always needed them. Then I found the world headquarters for shims right under our noses! From his little enclave in southeastern Manitoba, Dunlop made shims by the millions and shipped them across North America.

Dunlop sold his equipment and shim contracts four years ago to an American outfit. Now the world headquarters for shim-making is in the United States unfortunately, like so many things. That makes the story dated and so I haven't included the story here. I've tried to update other stories where it seemed needed.

I've toured a lot of interesting rural homes — from those elegant Eaton catalogue models to a house that one ambitious couple from MacGregor built right into a hill. I've seen some of the most interesting cottages imaginable, including cottages 80 to 100 years old.

I'm fond of some of the history pieces I've gotten to write, like the survival story of John Pritchard, a talkative greenhorn from England who became lost for 40 days naked in the Manitoba wilderness in 1805, and the forgotten story of the Battle of Grand Coteau, a Manitoba 'cowboys and Indians' battle like you see in the Westerns with a loss of life much greater than the Battle of Seven Oaks. And then there was the story of Walter Zeiler, the last of the red-hot bootleggers. Talk about colourful. This guy made every room he was in seem small.

I have made this final selection to reflect the range of stories. The dates show when each story appeared in the *Winnipeg Free Press*. Where necessary, I have added an update at the end.

I hope you enjoy the book as much as I've enjoyed the last decade writing it.

Bill Redekop, July 2011

Showy Lady's Slipper at Brokenhead Wetland

Places

THE DRIVE-IN THEATRE THAT TIME FORGOT
July 30, 2004

KILLARNEY — Morley Myers has an idea what's killing drive-in movie theatres.

"Not as much passion," winks Myers, projectionist at the Shamrock Drive-In here, 230 kilometres southwest of Winnipeg.

"When I first started, the last two rows used to fill up. You knew darn well they weren't watching the movies."

But the passion of Dorothy Gibson, the Shamrock's owner the past 43 years, is what keeps this drive-in alive today.

"I wouldn't exactly say it's profitable. I wouldn't advise anyone to buy one," she laughs. "It's something I enjoy. Everyone has a hobby, and I don't drink or smoke, but I like doing this," said Gibson.

Gibson plays the part of local movie madam, driving around town in a white Cadillac. And for all those Dorothys in Manitoba who wonder who claimed the vanity licence plate that says "DOT," well, it's here. At age 78, going on 79, she's entitled.

Gibson is found making popcorn an hour before the gates open, on a recent Friday night when *The Stepford Wives* is showing. She still sells tickets and enjoys meeting everyone at the gate. "They all say, 'Hi, Dot.'"

The Shamrock Drive-In was built in 1954 or '55, and Gibson and her former husband bought it in 1959. "We changed it around in 1962," she said, but that was the last time it underwent major renovations.

Which is a big part of its charm.

The Shamrock Drive-in

"Of all the drive-ins I visited, it was the most vintage," said Sean Karow, of Karow Prime Films in Toronto, who has made a documentary on Canadian drive-ins called *Shining Stars*. Karow visited a dozen drive-ins across the country.

"Time has stopped still at that place," said Karow. For example, the Shamrock is the only drive-in that still has row on row of outdoor speaker boxes, 125 in total.

The speaker boxes have broken more than a few side windows when drivers forgot to remove them. "Sometimes the younger ones barrel out of here, and it takes their window off," Gibson said.

And yes, kids still try to sneak in by hiding in a car trunk.

"I caught kids of some friends of mine, but I never told their parents. Sometimes I get them to clean up after," she said. That entails walking the drive-in grounds with what Gibson calls "Morley's stick:" a sawed-off broom handle with a nail stuck in the end for picking up trash.

"I'm a former teacher and I still like kids," she said.

If a fight breaks out, she'll go out and tell combatants to get back in their cars or she'll call the police. "I know most of their parents. They better not give me lip," she said.

Myers, a retired farmer, has been the projectionist the past 25 years. "I don't know what I'd do without Morley," Gibson says on more than one occasion.

"The late nights are getting a little harder to take," said Myers, 72. "When I really don't like a movie, I repair speakers," he added, pointing to a pile of speaker boxes at his feet.

And when a film breaks, 40 to 50 honking cars let him know about it.

The cast-iron projector he operates looks like it belongs in a museum. It was second-hand when the drive-in first opened in the 1950s, but its picture is still as good as the images from modern projectors.

The projector lighting is made by old-fashioned carbon arc lighting, which is basically two carbon rods sparking. "It's like a controlled fire," said Karow. Chimney ducts run along the ceiling, carrying out the heat from the projector.

Karow was fortunate enough to capture a brilliant pink sunset behind the Shamrock's big screen in his documentary. On this night, a cloud cover hid the sunset but there was still the surrounding pastoral panorama.

Most surviving drive-ins in Canada are rural and family-owned. Movie theatre chains are trying to get out of them.

"The drive-ins that are closing down are on the outskirts of cities. As urban sprawl encroaches on them, it becomes more profitable to just sell the land for development," Karow said.

Existing rural drive-ins will likely remain for many years. It's just that no new ones are being built because the cost is too great, he said.

Gibson and her former husband eventually owned five drive-ins, including ones in Brandon and Morden. She only operates the Shamrock today.

"At first, it was a really good money-maker. Then came video and VCRs. Now, business is steady. We have a lot of Americans come over — we're only 10 minutes from the border — who have summer cottages on Killarney Lake," said Gibson.

Every family member has worked at the drive-in snack bar, including Gibson's three children and seven grandkids.

Tonight, granddaughter Dominique is getting stressed because things are not going according to Hoyle. She can't get the 7-Up to pour out of the soft-drink fountain.

"She's just like her father," Gibson says, referring to her son Rocky, who plans to run the drive-in whenever Dorothy decides to retire.

The drive-in season could be scaled down next year, however. Like many other businesses, the cool spring hurt revenues. The Shamrock had only 139 customers between the May long weekend and July 1. "That does not pay any bills," said Gibson. While business has rebounded nicely since then, she plans changes.

"I've decided next year we won't open until July. The weather patterns are changing, and we have to change with them."

Dorothy is a larger-than-life kind of a person. She ran that drive-in with such style and flair. She would have been profiled a dozen times by media if she had lived in the city.

The drive-in was at risk of closing in 2011, after Killarney Mayor Rick Pauls and his family had run it the previous two years. However, buyers were found in spring in Darren and Joanne Struss. Dot owned the Shamrock Drive-In for 51 years. Shamrock Drive-In movie listings can be found on Facebook. Movies run Thursday to Sunday for the summer. The theatre accepts cash only.

SNAKES ON THE PLAINS
July 27, 2008

DOUGLAS — In just three years since it opened, Westman Reptile Gardens has already starred in 15 movies.

Owners Dave and Candi Shelvey supplied Madagascar hissing cockroaches for the movie *Addicted*, land crabs for *The Haunting in Connecticut,* a king snake for *Who Loves the Sun* and rattlesnakes for *The Box Collector.*

For *The Lazarus Project*, they supplied the carpet python that slithers over actor

Paul Walker's body while Walker is strapped to a gurney.

For miniseries *Category 7: End of the World,* that ran on CBS in 2005, they supplied poison arrow frogs, tomato frogs, White's tree frogs and others. In the movie, some environmentalists hold a Frogs of the Amazon benefit dinner. But the

Dave Shelvey and an albino Burmese python

frogs escape and start killing their high-minded protectors. Nothing should be read into the fact it was shot in the Manitoba legislature.

But the cutest role, if there is anything cute in the Shelveys' collection, was for the recent movie version of Margaret Laurence's *Stone Angel.* There's a scene in the movie where the young Hagar Shipley character played by Christine Horne discovers ants crawling up her leg. The producers thought local red ants would suffice. But the ants kept biting Horne, and she was becoming increasingly annoyed.

So someone picked up the hotline to Dave and Candi. Dave arrived with non-biting black harvester ants — they have tongues so the only risk is being ant-licked — from south-central United States. Dave dumped the ants onto a sheet of cardboard. Vaseline was rubbed onto Horne's leg. Dave pinged the back of the cardboard, the ants sailed through the air onto Horne's leg, "and they got the shot," said Dave.

Dave usually works as a stunt double to handle his creatures in movies. "They don't want to risk injury to the actors so they stick Dave in there," said Candi. Rock musician Alice Cooper has also borrowed their snakes when performing in Canada because he can't get his own across the border.

If you haven't heard of the Westman Reptile Gardens, it's time you did. It's a revelation. No one expects to find a first-class display of the largest collection of reptiles and creepy bugs in Canada in the middle of a mostly empty prairie. The collection is larger than that at the San Diego Zoo in fact, "we're not far from taking the North American title," said Dave.

Some people in the area had concerns when Dave, 38, built his reptile gardens in farm country just off the Trans-Canada Highway, east of Brandon. Someone wondered what would happen if there was a fire. Would all the creatures, including 17 crocodiles and 1,400 snakes, run amok, terrorizing the countryside as they do in the Hollywood disaster movies the Shelveys work on?

Dave assured everyone the reptiles are securely penned and would not escape in a fire.

The museum seems more like a sanctuary for that part of nature we find hardest to love. The first thing you see upon entering is a cobra snakehead inside a large tank. Chances are it spotted you first, eyeing you up as if sizing up dinner.

The cobra snakehead is just the most vicious fish on the planet. It kills piranhas. It once jumped out of the water and tried to bite Dave's hand off. Dave feeds it dead field mice.

If that's not enough introduction — and you're just in the gift shop to start — there's a cork board on the other side of the door with photos of some of Dave's bloodier bites.

"We call it the 'gore board'," said Candi. One is a 17-stitch bite on Dave's pinkie from an albino Burmese python. The python is known as more of a hugger but also has four rows of teeth on top and two rows on the bottom.

"When they grab on, they lock on, and you can't get them off. You have to have patience and wait five minutes until it lets go," explained Dave, who estimated he has needed more than 500 stitches since he started collecting reptiles as a kid.

You've still only gone two steps into the museum.

On the lighter side, just before you enter the actual exhibits, you see that for $5 you can have your picture taken with a live six-metre python wrapped around your neck — not quite wrapped like a scarf, mind you, more like an unknotted necktie.

Uh, maybe next time.

Some people don't get past the entrance. Dave said men are just as likely as women to be scared off. When school children from a Hutterite colony toured, the girls went through but all the boys refused.

What a collection.

There's Doc, an African dwarf crocodile who at 2.3 metres is the longest ever measured. There's Mikey, a 2.8-metre American alligator. There's a 5.2- metre African rock python.

Westman Gardens has the only two Nile crocodiles, the second-largest species of crocodile in the world, on display in Canada.

There's the soft-shell twist-neck turtle that pulls its head into its shell sideways instead of straight back and Felix, the soft-shell turtle whose shell is malleable, like rubber.

There are also 12 different types of cockroaches and four different millipedes, including a giant African millipede that looks like a cigar that runs away when you reach for it. There's a marine toad that people lick to get stoned, a leopard gecko and Brazilian death head cockroaches. There's an Amazonian giant tarantula, called the Goliath bird-eater, which reaches 30 centimetres. There are baby albino clawed frogs from Africa.

Housing the bugs and reptiles took some good old prairie ingenuity. Dave was quoted a price of $180,000 for construction of a small building with enclosures for his critters.

Then the German military pulled out of its Shilo base, and Dave purchased the barracks for $1. (It cost $18,000 to move it.) The building was ideal and twice the size of the $180,000 one.

He re-fashioned the barracks into a facility similar to the ones at the Assiniboine Zoo for cold-blooded creatures. It's also geothermal, which saves mega energy considering reptiles have to be kept at 26.6° C year-round.

Candi was overjoyed when Dave completed the structure, because it meant getting the critters out of the house.

Dave already had a large collection of reptiles when he met Candi. From time to time, that became an issue. "She asked me several times if it was her or the animals, which would I choose? I'd say, 'See ya,' and she'd say, 'You could have at least taken a minute to think about it.'"

Candi, outgoing and people-oriented, is company spokeswoman and is currently lobbying their local council and the province to approve better highway signs for Westman Reptile Gardens. Signage is very poor for a museum of its magnitude.

Dave prefers hanging with the reptiles over people projects. He also runs Dave's Reptiles and Stuff, which is involved in the wholesale trade.

Gift shop souvenirs include concrete garden snakes — a more sinister take on the traditional garden gnome — and glass paperweights embedded with scorpion, tarantula or preying mantis.

Westman Reptile Gardens receives 15,000 visitors per year. It's open year-round, Monday to Saturday from 10 a.m. until 8 p.m., and Sundays and holidays from noon to 5 p.m. Admission is $5 for adults, $3 for kids ages 3-15. To get there, turn south off Trans-Canada at Highway 340, and west on Thompson Road.

I can never say enough about the Westman Reptile Gardens.

I went back a second time, this time with my son, Ethan, and we were lucky enough to arrive at feeding time, which is just once a week for many of the critters. We saw a crocodile pick up its dead rabbit, and just freeze, as if it wasn't going to eat while people were watching. You'd think that after not eating for a week the crocodile would just chow it down in two gulps, but it just stood there with the bunny in its jaws. Perhaps it was just savouring the moment.

People visiting the area should also see the Royal Canadian Artillery Museum just 15 minutes away in Shilo.

WILD ABOUT ORCHIDS
July 21, 2003

GULL LAKE — "These are my girlfriends," said Bud Ewacha, pointing out some of the wild orchids in the Brokenhead Wetland.

With tart-sounding names like 'Rose Pogonia' and 'Showy Lady's Slipper,' you'd think he'd met them in a Wild West saloon.

These beauties are all dolled up. They are part of a wetland so rich in

Bud Ewacha at Brokenhead Wetland

wild orchids and carnivorous plants that it could become the province's 17th protected reserve, the highest level of protection afforded habitat in Manitoba.

Ewacha, president of the Conserve Native Plants Society, provided a recent tour.

It's a truly amazing place. Walk on top of this wetland — it's comprised of a thick sedge of plants and grasses that sit on top the water — and it feels like you're walking on a water bed. You can actually bounce the floor of floating plant material that spreads over a vast marsh.

The wetland contains 28 wild orchids, many of them rare, and 8 of the 10 insect-eating plants native to Manitoba.

Many of the orchids are small and may be hard for the untrained eye to spot. The largest orchids are the Showy Lady's Slipper, the Yellow Lady's Slipper,

A Pitcher plant

and Moccasin flower. The orchid season starts in late May and is nearly over by mid-July.

There are other fascinating plants. Labrador Tea grows in abundance. "You can actually drink it, but it's not too good. Don't drink too much or you might have to find a washroom," said Ewacha.

Then there are the insect-eating plants. They're not giant, like in the comic books, or have teeth, like in B movies. The one we examined is the Pitcher plant. Its leaves curl into tubes that were filled like shot glasses from a recent rain. The insects crawl into the tubes and become trapped in the tiny hairs. We could see tiny flea carcasses Velcro-ed to the insides. The plant dissolves the insects for nourishment.

There is also something called golden thread that is licensed in the United States as a pharmaceutical plant.

Some other biota include Round Sundew and Spatula Sundew. There is cranberry-red moss up to a foot thick in some places.

The wetland is just 50 or so metres north of the junction of PR 59 and PR 304 on the west side. To reach it requires a short jaunt along rough trails through a sort of enchanted forest of spongy earth, twisting cedar trees, and some peculiar holes in the ground large enough for you to imagine a hobbit living down there.

At the wetland, visitors need rubber boots and should avoid open water. Ewacha said he once plunged a stick over two metres down one of the open pools. People should also wear mosquito netting.

One of the threats to the wetland is the possible future twinning of PR 59. Protected ecological reserve status would require the highway be twinned away from the wetland.

"It's one of the most important fens [a marsh fed by an underground stream] in the world," said Ewacha, who has lobbied for the fen's protection since 1995. Ewacha said he successfully defended the wetland when some cottagers from nearby Gull Lake wanted to draw its water years earlier.

The province agrees the fen is important. "We're working hard to set it aside," said Helios Fernandez, Manitoba Conservation's ecological reserves specialist. "It's a very distinctive area, and certainly worthy of protection."

The Conserve Native Plants Society would also like the province to lay down boardwalks and plaques explaining what visitors to the wetland are seeing.

Fernandez said protected status and a boardwalk are separate issues. The province will consider a trail system only after it obtains protected status for the wetland, he said.

The province must first consult with Brokenhead First Nation. The wetland borders the first nation's reserve and it is government policy to consult with first nations.

Bud Ewacha, who passed away in 2011, was a bit of a rogue orchid lover. He founded the Native Orchid Conservation Inc. in 1998 but by 2002 was removed from the board in a membership vote. So he founded a new organization, Conserve Native Plants Society. Regardless, no one would argue Bud's heart wasn't in the right place. I'm grateful to him for showing me this amazing site.

The work of orchid lovers was soon successful. In 2005, a 563-hectare section of the Brokenhead Wetlands was declared an ecological reserve by the provincial government. Work is being done now to make it more accessible to the public.

Doris Ames, president of Native Orchid Conservation Inc., wrote in an email: "For the last few years representatives from Native Orchid Conservation Inc, the Brokenhead Ojibway Nation and the Manitoba Model Forest have been working on planning and fundraising for a system of trails and boardwalks so people can visit this unique area safely and without damaging the rare orchids and other plants.

"This is an expensive project but we have some money together now and hope to start brushing and building the first section of the trail and parking lot this spring [2011]."

STUMPED!
June 25, 2010

SANDILANDS — A chump stumped by a stump?

That described yours truly tromping through the woods last week in search of the "Giant Stump." Readers advised me I would find this mystery object east of Winnipeg along the Trans-Canada Highway.

Two emails arrived within a week telling of a mysterious giant stump. It wasn't real. It was made of concrete and perhaps some kind of fibreglass composite exterior.

But it was off in the middle of nowhere. And it was massive, three metres across.

Problem was the directions in the emails didn't match. One said the stump was just east of Richer. Another said it was just west of the Spruce Siding turnoff, or about 25 kilometres east of Richer in the Sandilands Provincial Forest.

Giant tree stump

One set of directions said there was "a little path" to the giant stump. The other said there was "an old trail." One said it was 100 metres off the highway, the other said it was 100 feet.

Perhaps most confusing, one placed the giant stump where the Trans-Canada is split by a woody strip. The other placed it where the Trans-Canada is split by a woods a *second* time.

I began at the first location. Like reading a great novel, the unessential discoveries you make on a nature walk are often what make it great, not necessarily the big theme.

I didn't see the stump there but found something else. I didn't know ditches could be so interesting! Orchids beautiful enough to pop into your mouth like barley candy grew there.

I found a large yellow lady slipper and thought how unique and beautiful, only to walk a little ways and see they were as common as dandelions.

I also found decades of human detritus. It was like an archeological dig with your foot. You could kick them up with the toe of your sneaker: a screwdriver handle, a set of lock-grip pliers, two non-matching work gloves, drink cans, all in just a square metre patch of ground. They were concealed in shallow graves under decades of wind-blown dirt and highway dust.

But no stump.

On my second stop, I walked a trail in the woods that ran alongside the ditch. It was an animal trail. I walked a long way, occasionally veering into the woods along fainter trails. I half expected to meet up with some creature using the trail. 'Hello, Mr. Bear. Do I have the right of way? Never mind. After you. No, I insist. After you.' It doesn't take much time to start feeling like you're changing somehow, becoming a smidgen like Henry David Thoreau, walking alongside the woods on an animal trail. Especially on work time.

Wild roses were starting to blossom, and the entire kingdom of flying insects, with their different tones and decibel levels buzzing, were out but they were too busy enjoying their first days of life to bother with me.

But still no giant stump.

So I headed back to the car. I couldn't think of an excuse to account for anymore of my time spent on this. I'd parked on a little sand road off the highway and before getting back on the highway, decided to see where it went. It was just one last pinch of curiosity. I wasn't even thinking of the stump anymore. Nobody said it was down a road, or at least a sand road. I turned left down the vehicle trail covered with that type of ground-crawling vegetation that grows in sand.

And I drove the trail right up to the giant stump. It was impressive. It was about stomach high. It's outer bark was attractively creviced and painted grey.

One emailer had thought it was a base for an old fire tower.

Nature photographer Hans Arnold — he runs Hans Arnold Photography and his book, *Wish You Were Here* (out of print) was a bestseller — had another explanation. He was the first to alert me to the stump, stumbling on it while looking for things to photograph.

He said he met a retired Manitoba Conservation officer at a function and asked about the stump. The retired officer said the stump was built to hold a giant statue of Smokey the Bear to warn about forest fires. That was in the late 1960s, early 1970s.

A provincial spokesman filled in the rest of the story. A fire had blazed through Sandilands Forest in the fall of 1955. So the province began building the statue while that stretch of the Trans-Canada was being converted from a two-lane to a four-lane highway.

Two summer students built the stump. Then the federal government changed its mind about the placement of the new Trans-Canada. Officials decided to reroute it about 100 metres farther north. That was too far away for motorists to see Smokey and the project was abandoned.

The stump is pretty easy to find. Driving east, there's a yellow seasonal sign where the sand road begins that reads: "Zack's Burger Bus 7 Kms Ahead."

I was feeling a little hungry myself after all that walking but Zack's wasn't open during the week. I headed to Geppetto's for a bite from its snack shop, and, so it felt, back to my regular job and life.

TOUR GUIDE A TIRELESS CRUSADER FOR HIS FEETLESS FRIENDS
October 2, 2001

NARCISSE — What would you get if Ed Wasserman fell into a pit of 70,000 wriggling garter snakes?

Answer: A lot of happy conservation officers.

Wasserman is the affable tour guide at the Narcisse snake dens, about 100 kilometres north of Winnipeg.

But Wasserman is also a royal pain in the asp for Manitoba Conservation. He's like one of those party noisemakers — the kind that uncoil like a snake — constantly blowing in the department's ear.

Snake man Ed Wasserman

Den of garter snakes

This year, Manitoba Hydro voluntarily installed nine underground culverts so snakes could cross Highway 17 without getting killed. But it was Wasserman who made all the noise about it, pleading several times in the *Free Press* on behalf of the snakes.

Two years ago, Manitoba Conservation put up low ditch fences, also to prevent snake fatalities, but only after constant brow-beating from Wasserman.

"My picture's probably up on every dart board in every Manitoba Conservation office," Wasserman says.

"Ed is a bit of complainer but it's based on his strong dedication to the site," MLA Tom Nevakshonoff (Interlake) starts out saying in an interview.

But by midpoint in the interview, the diplomatic veil starts to slip and Nevakshonoff says that Wasserman "can be abrasive and trying at times with some of our staff." By interview's end, Nevakshonoff is saying things like, "It's never enough for Ed."

Who is Ed Wasserman, protectorate of, champion for, Manitoba's garter snake?

"I'm from the north end. Isn't everybody?" shrugs Wasserman.

Wasserman moved out to the Interlake 15 years ago. He operates an appliance repair business from Narcisse, mostly for commercial buildings in Winnipeg.

"It's the old turn. People from the country want to move to the city, and people from the city want to move to the country.

"There are people out here who think I'm nuts. They've lived out here with the snakes all their lives and don't see them as anything special. But me, when I moved out here I was fascinated with the snakes from day one."

On his tours, Wasserman encourages snake-viewing as a tactile experience. "Pick it up, pick it up," he instructs. "Now, use two hands and let it go from hand to hand like a slinky."

"If people hold a snake," he explains, "they've made a friend for life and they won't stomp on one next time they see it."

A visitor from Ireland, not knowing that the Snake Man is in earshot, says she isn't overly impressed — the snakes are a little sluggish in the morning until it warms up. So Wasserman gets her son to hand the woman a snake. She proceeds to drop it, jump backward, and stands frozen with heels and knees pressed together, making a face like she just bit into the wrong type of mushroom.

The snakes may nip you the odd time, says Wasserman, but not hard enough to break your skin. So even if you fell into one of the snake dens, you wouldn't be harmed. Earlier this year, an international film crew from India had its host lie down while the crew laid snakes on top of him.

Other visitors this year have included a still photographer from Paris; an Israeli travel show; film crews from France, Germany, and Yorkshire Television in England. Last week, CBC's *On the Road*, hosted by Wayne Rostad, spent three days filming the site. Rostad did not have snakes laid on top of him.

The site attracts snakes for its cracks and fissures in the limestone bedrock that snakes can slither down to hibernate. It nests about 70,000 snakes at this time of year — the biggest concentration of snakes in the world, Wasserman says.

Wasserman's latest crusade is to get more Manitoba Conservation funding so the site is maintained in the fall. That could include fall guides, as well. Currently, the department only funds the site for six weeks in spring, when the snakes mate in large, orgiastic mating balls. After spring mating, the snakes leave the dens for the sloughs and marshes in the area.

But the snakes return after birthing in mid- to late-August, and hang around until about the first week of October before slipping down the limestone cracks to hibernate.

"No one seems to know that the best time for viewing is in the fall. In the spring, it's all muddy and there are mosquitoes out," says Wasserman.

SANDY LAKE MAN KEEPS THE TRAINS A-ROLLIN'
February 14, 2011

SANDY LAKE — When Earl Symonds was a child living upstairs of the Sandy Lake train station where his father was agent, crews would frequently give him rides.

"Railroaders in those days loved kids," Symonds recalled. "A train would come along and someone would holler out the window, 'Elsie [his mother], we're taking Earl to Rossburn and back.' It was an hour and a half there and an hour and a half back, and I loved it."

Today, the crew would be suspended for violating Article 15, Section 31 of the Something Act; RCMP would warn the family about sexual predators; and Child and Family Services would intervene on grounds of parental neglect.

Fortunately, kids were freer back then and Symonds developed only one major psychological disorder: model railroader.

He can run up to 18 model trains at once in his basement. His model engine has pulled up to 100 cars. There are 915 metres of track, like Frankenstein's stitches, crossing every flat surface downstairs. There are 20 tunnels through mountain ranges (there are always mountain ranges), and about a dozen bridges over canyons.

"I'm addicted. Pepsi, rum and model railroads," he said, inviting the scribe to join him in a drink.

It can take up to four minutes for one train to go around the basement. The longest track traverses three bridges and 12 tunnels, including a lengthy tunnel that runs through the larder where he keeps his canned goods, past a shelf where Symonds stores the liquor and emerges at about the sixth step on the basement stairs, before continuing around the basement perimeter.

He's got eight speakers under tables and in the rafters providing 18 different railroad sounds, from the ding-ding-ding of crossing gates, to the clickety-clack noise wheels make on tracks, to train whistles.

"I've got about 500 engines, 1,500 freight cars and 300 passengers cars. What can you do when you're addicted?"

Model railroader Earl Symonds

In 1967, Symonds put his model railroad into a bus and toured the province as a travelling museum. It made national news. He put it back into the house and in 1990, made it a private museum, charging people $4 admission. His residence is less like a house, more like a house of worship to trains. About 600 people visit per year, he said.

"Earl has a wonderful model railroad and collection of railroad memorabilia," said Morgan Turney, editor of *Canadian Railway Modeller* magazine. "Unfortunately, he lives out in the boonies and there aren't a lot of people around to see it."

Sandy Lake is about 250 kilometres northwest of Winnipeg, near Riding Mountain National Park.

One prized possession is a replica of No. 6043, the last CNR steam locomotive on display in Assiniboine Park. Its last run was from The Pas to Winnipeg on April 25, 1960.

The number of model railroaders is shrinking. "It's a great hobby, but with the Internet and video games and texting, kids today aren't interested anymore. They want something where they can sit and push buttons," said Turney, who publishes the bi-monthly model railroader magazine out of Winnipeg.

"You've got to have a hobby," said Symonds. "I don't understand people who sit all day and do this [twiddles his thumbs]."

Model railroading isn't just running trains in circles. There are the different cars (he even has cars with graffiti), little people, many industrial scenes. Symonds has 200 track switches, 100 of which are automatic. He is getting up in years and would sell if made a reasonable offer.

"It was train crazy" living in the train station with his family and having trains arrive all hours of the day and night.

Railroaders nicknamed him Dimples. "I learned how to message by telegraph when I was nine years old."

Naturally, Symonds made a career at CN Rail. He started as assistant agent in Grand Beach. He was put in charge of closing train stations in the 1970s. The first station he had to close? Sandy Lake. "That was my father's station!" he said, although his father was long retired by then.

"Somebody had to do it," Symonds said.

You can find his museum by the sign in his front yard on the route into Sandy Lake.

LIGHT OF AUTHOR'S LIFE LIES IN PRAIRIE GRAVE
February 2, 2002

As anyone who knows me knows, I am a huge fan of the late writer, Frederick Philip Grove. I've written about him three times. Here are two stories, plus a detailed route to follow in Grove's footsteps.

RAPID CITY — I didn't know she died, I thought, looking at the gravestone and the panorama of the Little Saskatchewan River Valley behind it.

A trail through the snow led to the gravesite of Frederick Philip Grove, Manitoba's most famous male writer, in the southwest corner of the Rapid City cemetery, just north of Brandon.

Beside his gravestone was that of his daughter, who died in 1927. Her father died in 1948.

For me, May Grove was forever the fair-haired infant girl in *Over Prairie Trails*, Grove's first book, published in 1922. Every weekend, her father made an exhausting 55-kilometre trip in horse-drawn wagon or cutter sleigh to see her and her mother, his wife.

"And there on the porch stood the tall, young smiling woman, and at her knee the fairest-haired girl in all the world," Grove wrote.

Over Prairie Trails covers the period 1917–18. Grove was a school principal in Gladstone, while his wife and daughter lived 55 kilometres north in Falmouth, a village that no longer exists, where his wife taught.

Grove made the trip 36 times across Big Marsh country that school year. *Over Prairie Trails* is an account of seven of those trips. The book is one of the first naturalist descriptions of early Manitoba.

May Grove was two years old at the time. "Children are among the most effective means devised by Nature to delude us into living on," Grove observed on one difficult trip.

The book also marks the first time I've ever seen this description of Manitoba snowdrifts: mammiferous! He says it twice! Perhaps Manitoba could change its image. Our snowbanks could become breast-shaped and

Catherine, Phyllis May and Frederick Philip Grove

Alvin Suderman and Calvin Baker by the former Falmouth School

our bumpy Canadian Shield buttocks-ous.

People often advised Grove not to make the trip. It would be -34° C, or it was a blizzard, or a blizzard had passed through the day before and the snow was too deep for the horses. But Grove went.

He ran his horses through banks so deep it covered their heads. The horses got lost in the dark in frigid temperatures. But each chapter ends with a candle in the window of his prairie home.

The family lived in Rapid City from 1922 to 1929. *Over Prairie Trails* was followed by fiction works *The Turn of the Year* in 1923, *Settlers in the Marsh* in 1925, and *A Search for America* in 1927.

Then May died. "It was a tragedy, it was just such a tragedy," recalls former Rapid City resident Dorothy Young, now 86, living in a seniors' home in Brandon.

May's appendix burst. She was just 12 years old. Young was seven at the time.

"The family had her in the house in a casket down by the river. It was peony season, and we walked down to the house and took flowers. She was the first dead person I had ever seen."

In *Over Prairie Trails*, Grove stops and tries to imagine life without May. "The outlook without her was night. Such a life was not to be lived."

Young describes Fred Grove as "kind of different."

"He wasn't such a nice person. When he was writing, he would have a hard time. He would get mail, and it would be another rejection, and he would go up to his room and be so mad."

Publishers rejected *A Search for America* for more than 20 years before it was published and became his greatest book.

By contrast, his wife was very popular with both students and the community.

"I think he was really intense," said Margaret Northam, who with husband John runs a museum in Rapid City. "There were conflicting reports. Some people liked him, some didn't. I think he was probably a bit arrogant.

"But for people to write novels, they've got to be a bit different," Northam said.

There isn't enough space to relate Grove's adventurous life, but briefly: The red-haired Grove was born Felix Greve in Poland in 1879. He went to prison for fraud in the early 1900s and was deeply in debt when he fled to the United States in 1909. He worked on a farm near Fargo, N.D., in 1912.

He heard Manitoba needed teachers and passed himself off as one. His knowledge of German got him a teaching job in Winkler, where he signed the register as "Fred Grove." There, he met and married a much younger Catherine Wiens.

He taught in various communities around Manitoba. The couple moved to near Simcoe, Ontario, in 1929, where they had a son named Leonard. Grove died there in 1948.

The death of his daughter is how Frederick Philip Grove came to be buried in Rapid City. He wanted to be buried beside her. His wife Catherine is also buried beside them but in an unmarked grave, a serious oversight, to be sure.

There's more about Grove and the region in an exceptional museum in the town, whose unheated walls I was allowed to view out of season. The museum is open from June to September.

AUTHOR LEFT SOME RED FACES
August 26, 2003

BIG GRASSIE MARSH — It's great that Manitoba's best known male writer, Frederick Philip Grove, wrote so many novels set in this poor, sparsely populated community north of the Yellowhead Highway, people here say.

But did he have to write that some people used to visit a prostitute — and use real names?

Ah, the perils of having a budding author in one's midst.

Grove, who died in 1948, is arguably the one male author from Manitoba who ranks with female writers like Carol Shields, Gabrielle Roy and Margaret Laurence. He was celebrated across Canada, receiving standing ovations at appearances in his later years.

Grove emigrated from Germany and lived near Big Grassie Marsh, about 165 kilometres northwest of Winnipeg, from July 1917 to July 1919. It had tremendous influence on him. He would write five books set here: *Settlers of the Marsh, The Yoke of Life, Tales from the Margin*, and non-fiction works, *Over Prairie Trails* and *The Turn of the Year*.

In truth, residents such as Calvin Baker are proud that Grove fell in love with this region and gave it such prominence in his works — more than any other locale.

But Grove's practice of using names of real people for his characters, or derivatives of real names, has led to speculation over the years.

He cleverly mixed names. The Big Grassie Marsh is north of the Town of Gladstone. In his works, Gladstone becomes Balfour. The real town of Gladstone is named after William Gladstone, a former British prime minister. Grove's fictional town of Balfour is named after another former British prime minister, Arthur Balfour.

In *Settlers of the Marsh*, hero Niels Lindstedt is being told the facts of life by a neighbour called Mr. Hahn. Local speculation is Hahn is a former real-life resident named Holm. There is also a character in the novel named

Kelm. In real life, Kelm lived next door to Holm.

In *Settlers*, the fictitious Hahn tells the hero that certain men see a prostitute, and rattles off surnames of real-life residents.

"He said [name withheld] visited loose women. Was that really true? I don't know," said Baker, the local Grove aficionado.

I recently joined Grove enthusiasts Alvin Suderman and Ernie Isaak of Winnipeg on a tour of "Grove country" that skirts Big Grassie Marsh. Suderman reconstructed the first known map tracing the route in Grove's first published work, *Over Prairie Trails* (1922).

"The route was actually 30½ miles [49 kilometres]," Suderman said. "Grove made a miscalculation."

Many people living along the route, now a series of gravel farm roads, have little knowledge of its literary history. Ian Watson, who farms just north of Gladstone, explained his grandfather was one of many immigrant farmers who moved here in 1905 from Iowa.

Further north, Beverly Wutke wasn't aware that, based on Suderman's investigation of landmarks from the book, her farm is the likely setting of Niels Lindstedt's homestead in *Settlers of the Marsh*. (Grove was very precise about landmarks.)

Edwin and Amanda Wiebe have preserved the abandoned Falmouth School and teacherage on their farm for almost four decades. It was converted into a truck garage before they obtained it. The province wanted to burn down the school when it widened Provincial Highway 261, but the Wiebes moved it to a safe place instead. It is located about 12 kilometres west of Amaranth on Provincial Road 261.

Why did Grove find his muse in this godforsaken land near the western shore of Lake Manitoba, where people scratch out livings on land that's either marshy or stony? One gets the feeling nature here is like the child only a mother could love.

But then it reaches up and yanks your heart out, Baker said.

"There's an appeal here. There's a kind of melancholy," said Baker, 54, who has lived here all his life.

The land is steeped in hardship and tragedy. One story is of a neighbour's boy who fell into a well, and all people could see was his hat floating on the surface. "My dad went down to retrieve the body," said Baker.

The Groves moved into this German community because they both spoke German and could teach close to one another. They could have taught together in Winnipeg, but Grove loved nature too much to leave the country and never did live in a city.

Grove was famously unpopular as a person. He is described as aloof, arrogant and irascible by many accounts. It seems his wife, Catherine Wiens of Steinbach, had all the charm in the world, and Grove none of it.

But a different story is told here.

"His students thought the world of him," said Baker.

Baker's father, Otto, was taught by Grove for one year at Ferguson School, about six kilometres north of Falmouth School, where Catherine Grove taught. This was in 1918–19, a year after *Over Prairie Trails*.

"My dad said kids would always ask Grove a question to get him going, and then he'd tell the most fascinating stories. My dad said he learned more from Grove than all the other teachers combined," said Baker.

Another story is of Grove scolding a resident for growing ornamental shrubs instead of indigenous plant life.

"His idea has come about," said Baker.

Grove was regarded as a very progressive teacher, and the province later hired him to tour Manitoba and give lectures on his teaching methods.

An excellent source of information on Grove's life in Manitoba is the book *Frederick Philip Grove*, by former University of Manitoba professor Margaret Scobie, published in 1973, and available at the Winnipeg Public Library.

Alvin Suderman generously provided directions to anyone wanting to follow in Grove's footsteps:

OVER PRAIRIE TRAILS
Following the path of Frederick Philip Grove

The Town of Gladstone just off Highway 16, is the starting point for someone wishing to follow the path described by Frederick Philip Grove in *Over Prairie Trails*. Find the main street in Gladstone heading north and cross the bridge over the Whitemouth River. The road continues north for one mile before it jogs to the left for approximately a half mile. Grove's trail continues north along the road for 9 miles before turning left again for one mile. This intersection is called Bell's Corner in Grove's book and was the dividing point of the two trails used by Grove — the short cut used in summer and the longer trail used in winter to avoid the treed area with deep snow drifts.

The summer trail turns north from Bell's Corner. At the next mile, one comes to Grove's aptly named Twelve Mile Bridge as this bridge is 12 miles from Gladstone. The trail continues north and three and a half miles north of the Twelve Mile Bridge one passes the farms referenced by Grove as the Half-Way Farms. These farms were approximately half way to his destination. Eight miles north of the Twelve Mile Bridge one comes to the site of the White Range Line House — the setting for Grove's novel *Settlers of the Marsh*. The trail turns east for one mile and crosses a bridge — also one of the landmarks in the book. From here on the original trail was a trackless path through the trees. One has to go two miles north and three miles east to join Grove's original trail which was along the ridge of dirt left from excavating a major drainage ditch. Grove followed this path north for four miles and turned west onto what is now Provincial Road 261. His destination was Falmouth School — a one-room school building where his wife was the teacher. The school is on the south side of the road and approximately 100 yards from the corner where Grove turned onto PR 261.

The winter trail was longer as Grove would cut northwest from Bell's Corner toward the town of Plumas. In bad weather he would stop in Plumas and use the livery stable to rest and care for his horses. He continued north on what is now Provincial Road 260. This took him through the village of

Waldersee. Once he reached PR 261, Grove turned straight east until he came to Falmouth School.

NOTE: *I have used Imperial measurements as the miles are easier to count on the map and anyone driving the route can count the cross roads as they are one mile apart.*

FAITH ENDURING
November 14, 2009

COOK'S CREEK — Even though it's on the map, and its name is on highway signs, and its name is even used as the place name for this story, there really is no Cook's Creek.

It's not a designated town, or village, or even a train stop, and it never was. It's not even a designated hamlet although there is a cluster of maybe 10 houses and a museum two kilometres past the Cook's Creek sign. The Cook's Creek most people know is just what they see at the road sign driving out from Winnipeg: a store (now closed) and an independent living centre.

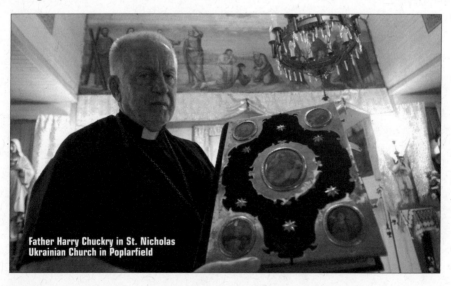

Father Harry Chuckry in St. Nicholas Ukrainian Church in Poplarfield

And a church. But what a church.

When you first spot Cook's Creek Ukrainian Immaculate Conception Church on the flat scruffy prairie, you may think you're hallucinating. You may want to rub your eyes. It's as if you'd stumbled on a lost Disney World. The building looks like it could become unmoored and start floating above the ground.

It's really more castle than church. It has nine large cupolas in the Ukrainian church style, not so much onion-shaped here as hemispherical, like ice-cream cones.

Neither are its colours the usual somber church colours. It's a pale yellow colour somewhere between late-day sunshine and a lemon lozenge. A candy colour. A happy church. The exterior design has many baroque curves and shapes, and blind arcades encircling the roof line. Be creative, they sermonize.

Inside, the walls are painted pastel green and yellow, and the ceiling pastel blue with black stars. Blue and yellow are the national colours of Ukraine. Mural-sized religious paintings dominate the front walls.

Its builder was Father Philip Ruh, a pipe-smoking priest and maker of some of the best moonshine east of Winnipeg. It was a different era. Many fathers and Fathers smoked a pipe, like early versions of *Father Knows Best*, and made homebrew to keep expenses down. "He was always known for having good stuff," parishioner Gerald Palidwor said, smiling, on a tour of the church.

More to the point, Ruh was the most influential architect of Ukrainian Catholic churches in Western Canada. He combined the Byzantine church architecture of Ukraine with the architecture of the great western European cathedrals to build some 40 churches, mostly in Western Canada. He was to the Ukrainian church what architect Joseph Senecal was to the Roman Catholic church and J.H.G. Russell was to Presbyterian churches in Western Canada.

But when Ruh first arrived at Cook's Creek on orders he build his next House of God here, he was underwhelmed, to say the least. There was nothing here. He had just come from building "prairie cathedrals" in Portage la Prairie (since razed) and Mountain Road, north of Neepawa (struck by lightning and burned to the ground in 1966). He'd moved beyond making dinky little churches for backwoods parishes you would

Ukrainian Catholic Church of the Immaculate Conception in Cook's Creek

think, and so he seemed to think.

"What a God-forsaken place this is," he said when he got to Cook's Creek, and wrote the bishop asking if there'd been some mistake. No, this was the will of God, the bishop replied.

So Ruh determined to build his legacy church. He began construction at the worst time, in 1930, just as the Great Depression was starting. The church would take 22 years to complete. It was built with all volunteer labour and parishioners' donations.

That included 20 boxcars filled with cement and thousands of tonnes of gravel and sand, all of it mixed by hand. "Youths were trained to handle saws and levels; men dug the foundation ditches; women hauled rocks; children carried smaller stones," wrote David Butterfield and Maureen Devanik Butterfield in their book, *If Walls Could Talk: Manitoba's Best Buildings Explored.*

The church construction took on no debt and was built entirely with hand tools. Ruh forbade any power tools, even a cement mixer. It was nearer to God that way. A pulley was the only modern machinery used, he told the *Winnipeg Free Press* at the consecration Sunday July 27, 1952. That opening service lasted five hours.

St. Mary's Ukrainian Catholic Church fire, August 19, 1966

And that was just for the church. There is also a grotto next door that Ruh patterned after the famous grotto in Lourdes. Grotto construction began in 1954. It was made with 23,110 bags of cement, 44 tonnes of steel, 6,592 yards of gravel. It wasn't completed until 1970 by the Knights of Columbus, eight years after Ruh died of cancer.

The grotto, with its tunnels, narrow stairs, and lookouts, feels medieval. You can almost hear monks' frocks swishing through its caves. It's a serene, pastoral place to wander, look out from, contemplate. Swallows forever dart through the cave openings, and volunteers forever have to wash away the swallow poop.

Yes, all amazing. But walking about you also notice something odd. You realize the church's exterior brickwork isn't brickwork at all. It's a concrete composite, dabbed with white spots and stenciled over with black lines to make it look like brickwork.

This pattern of imitation is found inside the church, too. The marble isn't marble but a kind of feathered paintwork to make the wooden arches look like marble. The grotto is concrete that has been shaped to look like the natural stones in Lourdes.

This artifice is curious for a church, and more curious considering Ruh shunned power tools for a greater authenticity.

Why did Ruh do this? Why did he feel he had to dress up some materials to look like something they weren't? Is this just found in Ruh churches or other Ukrainian churches as well?

It didn't add up to a Dan Brown mystery but it was a mystery nonetheless as I embarked on a tour of Ukrainian churches in rural Manitoba.

* * *

The tall rural Ukrainian Catholic or Ukrainian Orthodox churches break up the monotony of the countryside. With the mass demolition of grain elevators since the 1990s, the churches have taken over as sentinels of the prairie.

The Ukrainian churches, topped with their distinctive hemispherical or onion domes, stand out more than the steeples and towers of Roman Catholic and Anglican churches. They certainly stand out more than the relatively plain Mennonite or Methodist churches, where churchgoers are directed to pay attention to the "word," not the walls.

There is at least one central dome on a Ukrainian church, representing Jesus Christ. There can be any number of smaller satellite domes around it. If it is accompanied by two domes, that forms the Holy Trinity; four extra satellite domes represent evangelists Matthew, Mark, Luke and John; seven domes in total represent the sacraments: baptism, confirmation, holy eucharist, penance, holy orders, marriage, and extreme unction (last rites).

Most church's floor plans are cruciform — shaped, like a cross laid flat on the ground. The buildings have three chambers with the central chamber the largest and representing the cross piece. Inside the churches, the cross shape is outlined by red carpet that runs up the centre aisle.

The architecture is the Byzantine style the settlers brought with them from Ukraine, employing extravagant colours, shapes and curves. "They are fabulous buildings. They are powerful expressions of the peoples' culture and themselves," said David Butterfield, provincial architectural historian, in an interview.

Inside Cook's Creek church

"The artwork of the church was always to show some evidence of the kingdom of heaven," one priest explained.

You find it in the smallest 30-seater church like in Gardenton, east of Emerson, and in "prairie cathedrals" like Cook's Creek. Some churches, like the Holy Resurrection Church in Dauphin, now a museum, have virtually every expanse of wall and ceiling painted with ornamental designs and religious figures, called icons. The Dauphin church was brilliantly painted by Theodore Baran of Saskatoon, whose work enlivens over 70 Ukrainian Catholic churches mostly in Western Canada.

Baran wasn't afraid to add his own touches. In the Dauphin church, his Blessed Mary wears red boots like female Ukrainian dancers. She holds a towel with traditional Ukrainian embroidery.

One prominent painter of church interiors was Jacob Maydanak, a humourist-cartoonist by trade. Not only did he paint the interiors of Ukrainian churches such as Fisher Branch and Olha, but he recruited budding artists like Leo Mol to help. Mol's stained glass beautifies many Ukrainian churches in Winnipeg and the St. Mary's Ukrainian Catholic Church in Brandon. A man named Hnat Sych is famous for the marbling effects he painted on the timber walls of many churches. The churches point to an extraordinary pool of artistic talent among first and second generation Canadian Ukrainians.

Most mural-sized paintings were painted onto canvas and then mounted on the walls and ceilings. But at the Holy Ghost church in Sandy Lake, south of Riding Mountain, another famous church artist, Peter Lypinski, painted his icon right onto the ceiling, à la Michelangelo. The painting is of Mary and her ascension into heaven. She is surrounded by a multitude of cherubs and seraphs, and encased in fleecy, bedding-like clouds.

Lypinski used the method Michelangelo used. He sketched his painting onto brown paper. Then he pin-pricked the outline of his drawing, fixed it to the ceiling, and filled in the holes so the outline stayed on the ceiling. Then he painted the ceiling from a scaffold. It is the most beautiful ceiling painting I saw in any Ukrainian church.

But then you drive a little farther west to Olha, and stop at Olha General Store, where Marion Koltusky, who has run the store for 38 years, has the church key. You ask her to let you into the 104-year-old St. Michael the Archangel Church. She has a made-up sign ready to put in her store window: "I'm just in church with tourists. Be back shortly."

And you walk inside the church and it's time to haul out the thesaurus again because this one now seems like one of the most beautiful churches you've seen. The churches are never cookie cutter imitations of each other.

"There isn't one [Ukrainian church] you step into where you're not transformed," said Butterfield.

That makes them very, very hard to close.

I chose rural Ukrainian churches because they tend to be older and more historic than the urban churches. Many rural Ukrainian churches are 80, 90 or 100 years old and more, and are still in use. You will find them down dusty gravel roads with no highway number. Or you may stumble upon them while horribly lost and trying to find your way back to a main highway.

They've survived. They haven't closed the way many other churches have across rural Manitoba. Many churches of other faiths have been converted into pottery studios and music studios and craft stores and museums

Father Harry Chuckry in St. Nicholas Ukrainian Church

and private homes and even condos.

Still, Ukrainian congregations are getting very small and the members are aging. A number of the churches aren't keeping up bill payments to the archeparchy. The Ukrainian Catholic Archeparchy of Winnipeg has begun a travelling review of these small churches.

Father Richard Soo, Chancellor of the Archeparchy of Winnipeg, said the archeparchy doesn't want to close churches — that's up to parishioners — but said parishes have to attract new members. "The church is not a museum. It's not our mission to keep open architecturally interesting buildings," he said.

It's a difficult issue on all sides.

* * *

How spiritual they were. And how they sacrificed. People may deny the spiritual basis of these old churches — all old churches, regardless of denomination — but they cannot deny that they comprise a significant part of our shared history.

An example of the sacrifices made by settlers is the church at what's called Mountain Road, another place on the map named for an extraordinary church designed and built by Father Ruh. Mountain Road is a place name north of Neepawa along a scenic drive connecting Highway 5 and 10.

Parishioners put up their church in 11 months in 1924-25. The parishioners, largely farmers, put in at least 50 days of volunteer labour each into construction. Some worked up to 200 days. Each family had to donate at least one horse-drawn wagon load of gravel. They cut and hauled timber from nearby Riding Mountain, which wasn't yet a national park.

Once completed, the St. Mary's Ukrainian Catholic Church was the largest wooden structure in Canada. It was 39 metres to the top of the highest cross, or five times the height of a typical hip-roofed barn. It had six entrances, 17 doors, 130 windows. It was supported by 40 wooden columns. It was larger than even the Cook's Creek church.

"They didn't have to build that high or that big but the parishioners were so excited about it," said Louise Kostenchuk, who was married in the church. The parishioners were very proud of what they had built. The church attracted attention across North America, and even abroad, attested by guest book signings from visitors from places like South Africa, Norway, and the British Isles.

"These old churches were the one place where people tried to make a statement," said architectural historian Butterfield. "They are phenomenal expressions of a community's faith in the future and determination to honour its past."

George Kostenchuk, Louise's husband, remembers Friday, August 19, 1966. It was just after lunch. "There was just a little cloud in the sky. There was just a single lightning bolt. And it struck the church."

Jim Kolesar was working his field that day. "It was just drizzling rain a little bit. I was cultivating across from the church and was starting to get a little wet. There was no cab on the tractor in those days. So I stopped beside one of the granaries and I was standing in the doorway of the granary to keep out of the rain," he recalled.

He saw lightning hit the church's highest peak, the top of the cross, and drive it straight down through the church's main dome. Then it blew a patch of shingles about two feet square off the dome, apparently from the lightning's exit, Kolesar said.

Smoke started to rise out of the dome. Flames began to eat their way through the dry timber like a starved lion. Within two hours, the largest wooden building in Canada was ash.

Everyone turned out to watch helplessly as their dream church burned down. There were some tears and holding onto each other but mostly people were just numb.

"That was the heart of the community. Everything revolved around that church," said Louise Kostenchuk.

While a modest little church has replaced it, the original Mountain Road church still has an emotional hold on people. A local history book was published in 2004 called *Looking Back: A History of Mountain Road, 1904-2004*. Almost the entire book is about a church that hasn't existed for four decades.

* * *

Dauphin had a huge hailstorm on August 9, 2007. People always boast about the size of hail, like golf balls, like softballs, like small meteorites, etc., but no one was boasting about the damage done by this storm. It was the worst summer storm in a century for Dauphin, a city founded by Ukrainian settlers. Virtually every one of Dauphin's 3,500 homes suffered roof damage. On some, the hail broke the wood beneath the shingles. Some homeowners were still trying to get roofs repaired more than two years later, and roofers were run off their feet. The City of Dauphin alone filed claims in the $5 million range for its municipal buildings. Claims on vehicle damage approached $70 million.

Then roofers looked at some of the battered Ukrainian church dome roofs. No thanks. The roof of the new Ukrainian Catholic Church of Resurrection cost $600,000 to repair. It took an outfit from Saskatoon to fix it. Fortunately, the church was insured to the teeth. It's brand new gleaming copper domes reflected the clouds drifting by.

However, most Ukrainian churches in the area are smaller and don't have insurance coverage or money to fix their hail-damaged domes. The onion domes are often the most vulnerable part of the churches in terms of water leaks. A Ukrainian Orthodox church in Sifton, now operated as a heritage museum, was also hit by hail. When I visited, it had a dozen pails and basins and recyling bins strategically located in the church nave and sanctuary to catch the drips.

Sargie Katchur, 79, the volunteer caretaker whose two assistants died "and now it's just me," said it would cost $64,000 to fix and their insurance covers just 80 per cent. The small town has trouble scrounging up that kind of money.

And it's just hard to find anyone to do it.

Same for Dauphin's old Holy Resurrection Church, now a museum and a federally and provincially designated historical site. Father Ruh designed it, too. It has five domes. "We're having a very difficult time repairing the roof. No one wants to climb that roof and put up the big scaffolding," said Terri Genik, one of a committee that looks after the museum.

It's not just hail that churches have to worry about. Repairs and restoration are required as buildings age. The Cook's Creek church had its roof reshingled in 2001. It cost $90,000. It had its wide, expansive front steps redone. That cost $140,000. It had a new boiler put in for heating. That cost in the $100,000 range.

The congregation is managing. The Cook's Creek parish had 350 families in 1929. Parish membership dipped to just 50 families in the 1970s. A new priest came along and injected energy back into the church by bringing back young families with youth programs. The church is enjoying a revival with about 185 families, said parishioner Gerald Palidwor.

* * *

What if...? What if the beautiful, small rural Ukrainian churches all held open houses one weekend every summer? People could take driving tours and see inside these beautiful churches, minded by a volunteer or two, and even make donations to support the churches. It could get people to explore an area like the Parkland, outside Riding Mountain National Park, which has the greatest concentration of churches. Why should I be one of the few lucky ones to see so many? Locals might sell crafts or farm produce outside the churches to raise additional funds.

The public would also discover all these peculiar Ukrainian place names like Ozerna, Kosiw, Halicz and Zoria. It could be a major event in Manitoba. Summer drives combining history, art, geography and spirituality.

Because this story only scratches the surface of what's inside the churches. For example, many churches will have elaborate chandeliers. One of the grandest is in the old Ukrainian Catholic Church of Resurrection in Dauphin, now a heritage site. It's a 1,600-piece chandelier imported from the former Czechoslovakia.

Then there's all the wonderful old bell towers. Metro Lukie, a cantor for 43 years in Ukrainian Catholic churches north of Riding Mountain, pointed them out to me one afternoon, on a six-church, three-hour blitz exclusively on dust-billowing gravel roads. The bells at some of those churches are so heavy they will lift two or three men off the ground on the backswing, Lukie said.

Some parishioners expressed interest in the idea of an annual open house but priests, in general, weren't sure. One told me that people should come out for Sunday services if they want to see a church. There is also some concern that exposure could leave the churches open to vandalism. The churches are isolated and vulnerable.

No consensus emerged from asking people why Ukrainian churches have survived so much better than other churches. Maybe Ukrainians have been more stubborn. Maybe the churches are just too beautiful to throw away. Maybe succeeding generations have felt a responsibility to maintain these inheritances. From my conversations with Ukrainian Manitobans, there is little doubt that these churches, in addition to being religious buildings, also stand as symbols of the struggles and endurance of their ancestors.

What about Ruh and his imitation marble and masonry?

I found it wasn't just Ruh. Most old Ukrainian churches contain imitation stone. It seems to have been the style to replicate the churches of the homeland, even if you didn't have the materials. It said you don't have to have marble to have marble; you don't have to be rich to be rich.

It also said don't take yourself too seriously. By the end, I had warmed up to this artificial masonry. I even started to appreciate it as an art form.

Some of it is fantastically done. In the Mink River Holy Trinity Ukrainian Catholic Church, the fake marble is drizzled with red veins that give it an eery look. You can't help but think, that it represents the blood of Jesus Christ.

"They wanted marble and they couldn't afford marble, and they had to fake it. Lots of Ukrainian and Russian architecture, there's a bit of tradition of this, of making things out of stucco and painting them to look like something else," said Butterfield.

When I asked Chuckry, the Interlake priest, if having the wood panelling painted to look like marble in St. Mary's Ukrainian Catholic Church in Meleb made it better, he replied, "Oh, much better. Just wood panelling would look very plain."

But when I asked about the blue Christmas lights poking out of holes in the wood frame of the Dormition of Mary mural at the front, he allowed that "sometimes, there's a going overboard. Fortunately, they're not flashing, like Las Vegas."

Perhaps not surprisingly, formally trained architects in Winnipeg looked down on Ruh's work at the time.

Ruh was a self-taught architect. For that matter, he was a self-taught Ukrainian. He was born in 1883 in Alsace-Lorraine, then German territory and now in France. He always regarded himself as more German than French, and later in Canada changed his name from Roux to Ruh.

After he was ordained in 1910, the Roman Catholic Church assigned him to Ukraine. He adapted quickly to the Ukrainian language and culture, and remained in the Ukrainian church all his life. He came to Canada in 1913 and began missionary work in northern Alberta. There he began designing and building many small Ukrainian churches. That was his start.

Neither was he only a designer. He was also a builder and labourer on the churches, and there are many photos of him pushing a wheelbarrow.

You don't have to leave Winnipeg to see a Ruh church. There's a fine example, Holy Eucharist, at the corner of Munroe Avenue and Watt Street in East Kildonan. Its stained-glass windows were made by Leo Mol.

Today, Ruh's gravesite is memorialized with a special place of honour, surrounded by spruce trees, in the cemetery next to the Cook's Creek church. His right-hand men in church construction, master builders Mike Sawchuk and Michael Yanchynski, are buried beside him.

MANITOBA'S GEOGRAPHY INCLUDES A BIT OF EVERYTHING
November 19, 2001

ASSINIBOINE VALLEY – We're not valley people, or so I thought, gazing down into the Assiniboine River gorge.

We're prairie people, lake people, boreal people, even a little bit mountain people. We have a bit of everything, geography-wise, likewise with our economy. Maybe that should be our motto: Manitoba – A Bit of Everything.

Except valleys. I was interviewing farmer Don Armitage, who is raising cattle the natural way, on grass, instead of on a grain diet that speeds weight gain but weakens the animals' immune systems.

Some residents of Miniota look out over the Assiniboine Valley

Don Armitage raises cattle in the Assiniboine Valley

We were standing in the bottom of the Assiniboine Valley near Miniota among his grazing cattle. "Do the cattle go up there?" I asked, peering up at the top of the valley about 100 metres above us. I groaned after asking it, as if I was laying one more ridiculous city demand on the poor put-upon farmers: inspecting whether his animals had adequate scenery. I looked back at the deadpan faces of the cattle studying me like I was weird.

"Yeah, they do," Armitage smiled. "I'll take you up there."

Before that, he stopped on the slope of the valley to show me the now empty fieldstone house that Buzz Currie, perhaps the most savvy editor I've ever had the pleasure to work with at the *Free Press*, grew up in and still visits. The yard slopes past the house like a ski hill, as if you might keel over when you step off the deck, and it could explain Buzz's unique view of things (slanted).

Armitage then drove his pickup up the side of the valley. At the top, a greying sign said Armitage Lookout, and we didn't speak for a minute, while he gauged my reaction.

The Assiniboine Valley is 100 metres deep and 1.6 kilometres wide. Looking out, I didn't know what to make of it. The sight, one of grandeur, was foreign to my sensibilities.

I imagined if I lived here, this is where I'd have gone when angry at my parents, or to think about a certain girl in my class. I wondered if it was the first or second or third date before Armitage took his future wife to see the lookout.

Later, further west in the town of Shellmouth, I had another glimpse of the Assiniboine Valley. I had interviewed some women who are restoring a church, and was about to drive off when I noticed, lined up through the church's gothic windows, a magnificent crimson sunset over the Assiniboine Valley. I drove into the valley, and into the sunset, and saw two coyotes, which are numerous this year and taking down the deer, hunters say.

I had to keep going with this valley thing I was on. Manitoba Conservation officer Ken Kansas said the western edge of the province is grooved by valleys: the Assiniboine Valley, the Little Saskatchewan River Valley, the Shell River Valley, the Souris River Valley, the Swan River Valley, even the Valley River Valley (between the Duck and Riding mountains). To the south is the Pembina Valley. Kansas said I just had to turn down a few gravel roads.

One road was like riding a snake's back, up and down south along the Assiniboine to where Saskatchewan's Qu'Appelle Valley enters Manitoba. Then I drove north to see the Asessippi Park and the Shell River Valley. Vertiginous awe. The hills are bald-faced with forest growing in the grooves like sideburns.

These were real valleys, with steep sides and wide valley floors, not like the Red River Valley, which is really a misnomer. It's actually a former lake bottom and doesn't look anything like a valley, says James Teller, University of Manitoba geologist.

Glacial melt 10,000 years ago created rivers 5 to 10 times their size today, which carved up the landscape in a process that took a couple of thousand years, Teller said. Rushing water once ran to the top of these valleys, he said.

Most of the valleys peter out at about Brandon and people who live in the eastern half of the province may never know about them. Maybe there should be a tour bus, or a tour map, connecting the valleys so people can see them with some level of comprehension.

And maybe my slogan doesn't need any footnote after all: Manitoba – A Bit of Everything.

Neil Young performs at Winnipeg Concert Hall, 2010

People

LAST OF THE RED-HOT BOOTLEGGERS
August 20, 2001

BOISSEVAIN — It was 1932 and just before midnight.

There was no moon. Walter Zeiler never travelled under a moon.

Zeiler carried 24 bottles of rye whisky, 12 bottles per saddlebag that hung on either side of his bronco. "I wrapped the bottles in straw," he said.

The fence at the United States border was made of thick oak posts strung high with barbed wire. His bronco, named King, made its way through the forest that night as it had many times before. But this time, when it made the leap over the border fence, its back legs caught on the wire and made a loud twang.

"The American patrol shone a huge spotlight. It hit right on me. I started to go like hell."

Midnight rider. Ride, farm boy, ride.

"I was a bootlegger," Zeiler said.

Zeiler, 94, is one of the last of the rumrunners still alive from the era of alcohol prohibition 70 years ago.

Everyone wondered where Zeiler was getting all his money.

Walter Zeiler

"I went into Brandon and went into the [tailor's] shop and bought a silk shirt and tie and black suit, and no one could understand it," Zeiler said, with a laugh in his room at Westview

Lodge in Boissevain where he lives alone.

He then bought a brand new Nash Ambassador Sedan for $2,000. This was the Depression. Zeiler was still living on his parents' farm.

"The banker said, 'How the hell are you getting the money?' And I said, 'You and a hundred more would like to know.' No one knew what I was doing."

That included his father, whose farm near the Turtle Mountains was being kept afloat with cash from his son; his father believed Walter made the money from trap lines. Not even the RCMP officer, who took his meals at the Zeiler home and patrolled the road that ran past their homestead into the United States, knew where Walter was getting the money.

"We ate breakfast, lunch and supper with him [the Mountie] but at night . . ."

At night, Zeiler would carry out his covert business.

A man with bull-like strength all his life, he remains a large and imposing figure in the John Wayne mould. Zeiler's only apparent fraility is some loss of hearing. "I drove tractor all my life and did a lot of hunting with a .306 [calibre rifle]," he said apologetically.

Canadian prohibition extended into the 1920s, but Manitoba was one of the first provinces to end it in 1923 and introduce government-controlled liquor sales. American prohibition was more strict and lasted until 1933.

So Zeiler would run legally bought Canadian liquor into the United States from his father's farm, about 10 kilometres from the border. Zeiler, then 25, travelled in the dead of night but never if there was a full moon, and never if it had been snowing, because he would leave tracks.

"I'd met a man from Minot, North Dakota, who'd come up to Canada. He would give me a roll of American money to buy cases of rye whisky."

Zeiler picked up the liquor at the depot of the Canadian Northern Railway. Liquor was already government-regulated in Canada. Zeiler said an individual could receive up to 12 bottles a week. He put down his younger brother's name so he could get 24 bottles a week to sell.

He would ride home from the depot, stopping about a kilometre from his father's farm to hide the liquor in the bush.

He made weekly deliveries to the Minot man, pulling in $600 a week, an astronomical figure for the time.

"I went through the bush. I never took the roads. I knew that bush like the back of my hand. It was exciting," he said.

"I was taking a really big chance if I got caught. But I had a really fast bronco."

His bronco, King, "was an old strawberry roan," he said with a gleam. The roan came cheaply, only $12, because "he was wild and mean and almost killed two people." Zeiler and King became a team.

Zeiler was a little wild and could be mean, too. "I always wanted to be like those Texas Rangers whose pictures you saw in the magazines," he said.

"I could shoot a gun and I could drink. To me, drinking rye whisky was like water."

He was an amateur boxer with no training who once KO'd a visiting British boxer in an exhibition match.

"I could punch equally hard with both arms," he boasted. He once almost killed a man in a fight. A doctor told him if he'd punched his opponent one more time in the ribs, he would have pushed the man's ribs into the vital organs.

"I was kind of a wild jigger."

Zeiler never was caught, not even the night the U.S. border patrol gave chase.

He discontinued bootlegging when the snow fell, and the following year the U.S. lifted prohibition, ending his bootlegging days.

But that was not the end of Zeiler's extraordinary story. Next he told the story of a passionate love affair that spanned almost six decades.

It was time to settle down. He married and had four children with his first wife, Ivy, on a farm 11 kilometres south of Boissevain. Today he has seven children, and more grandchildren than he can keep track of, he says, including two grandchildren in Australia, and a granddaughter who's a Mountie in the Yukon.

Zeiler and his wife hired a young housekeeper in a scenario that sounds almost like Margaret Atwood's best-selling novel, *Alias Grace*. One evening the housekeeper entered his room, took off all her clothes and laid down with him.

"What could I do?" Zeiler says. "She said she always loved me."

His affair with housekeeper Beryl, 12 years his junior, continued but Zeiler would not leave his wife.

Meanwhile, Zeiler's younger brother, who farmed down the road, proposed to Beryl. She accepted, with one proviso. "She told him she would marry him but she'd always love me."

Zeiler is asked several times if he wanted this part of his story printed. He insisted that he did. He said as the last survivor of the people involved, it was past time when anyone could be hurt by the account.

"It's the truth," he said on more than one occasion.

Beryl had two children with Zeiler's brother. Then Zeiler's wife, Ivy, became sick and died of tuberculosis.

Zeiler never stopped seeing Beryl. They would meet midway on a forested road between their farms. Then in 1952, his brother was killed in a farm accident when the tractor he was steering rolled on top of him. Seven months after the funeral — and 14 years after they first met — Beryl and Walter were married.

They spent the next 45 years together.

"We loved each other. No matter what we did, we worked as a team. We baled hay together, we threw hay in the loft, we milked cows together. It was a real team all our lives until she got Parkinson's Disease."

She died about four years ago. Staff at the nursing home where she spent her last years say Zeiler went to see her every day.

"I still dream of her. I thought she was here last night. I reached over on her side of the bed, but the bed was empty."

Zeiler says the other bootleggers he knew have also passed away, including a man who used to run the pool hall.

"I could go into his pool room and have a shot of whisky for nothing, any time I wanted," he said.

"I've enjoyed life," he said, shaking hands heartily, then grabbed his walker and made his way down the hallway to have lunch in the community dining room.

Walter Zeiler made every room he was in seem too small. He died in 2006 at age 99.

YOUNG AT HEART
April 10, 2006

CYPRESS RIVER — The wind sails and sails, with nothing to block it, on this rise overlooking a hilly prairie.

This is the prairie wind, and the *Prairie Wind* singer-songwriter Neil Young sings of on the title track of his new recording.

"It just really blows here. It blows harder up here than anywhere around," says a cousin of the performer, also named Neil Young, who lives in one of the original homes built by the Young clan from which the two Neils are descended. The family were Scottish immigrants who settled here in 1879.

Singer Neil Young's cousin Neil Young at heritage family home

Neil Young performing in Winnipeg

"He sure named the album right," adds another cousin, Greg Young, who lives down the road.

The Young families here — and the area is loaded with them — got a pleasant surprise recently when their famous cousin made known his connection to Cypress River, both the village and the creek, 140 kilometres southwest of Winnipeg.

On the title track of *Prairie Wind*, Young sings: "Tryin' to remember what my daddy said, Before too much time took away his head, He said we're goin' back and I'll show you what I'm talkin' about, Goin' back to Cypress River, back to the old farm house."

A recent story in *Macleans* magazine was probably correct in saying one shouldn't make too much of place names in Young's songs, where "memory and imagination merge to make romance."

But the *Macleans'* writer, in a story titled "Neil's Prairie Mirage", could not have been more wrong in his disparagement of Young's evoking the prairie wind.

"Toronto Wind, or even Winnipeg Wind, wouldn't have quite the same ring. Ever since Neil left Winnipeg at 19, seeking his rock 'n' roll fortune in a 1948 Buick Roadmaster hearse headed east on the Trans-Canada Highway, he has been on a mission of self-mythology," said *Macleans*.

Well, people here like to think they're more than a myth.

Even that high, quavering tenor voice Neil Young has made so famous, that near-falsetto he somehow squeezed into rock and roll music, and later country and folk music, has its home here. It's genetic.

"There are a lot of beautiful, beautiful singers in the Young family, and most of them have that high tenor voice that Neil has," said Marjorie Young, a cousin in Cypress River. "It seems to be a family characteristic."

Prairie Wind is dedicated to Neil's dad, Scott Young, a famous sportswriter and author who started his career as a *Winnipeg Free Press* copy boy. Scott Young was born in Cypress River in 1918, and died in 2005 in Kingston, Ontario.

Family like to tell the story of how someone came across Scott one day sitting outside on the school steps. Why wasn't he in class? the person asked Scott. He'd been kicked out for arguing with the English teacher, he explained. He was only in Grade 5 or 6.

Three songs on the album recall Young's fondness for this prairie region that he only visited as a kid, but which his father frequently came back to. Relatives interviewed said Cypress River has always been the home base where Young family members return.

"The whole idea of Cypress River, really, it always comes back to that. That's where all the uncles and aunts and grandparents, and my dad, too, are buried," said Dorothy Liss, Young's aunt and his dad's sister, who now lives in Winnipeg.

She thinks it has similar meaning for her famous nephew. Gushes Liss, 80, about Neil Young's CD: "It's a great record. It surely is."

* * *

In 1879, three Young brothers and some sisters — no one interviewed was certain how many — settled here. The Youngs were originally from Scotland, and lived briefly in London before immigrating as soldiers to Perth in Upper Canada in the early- to mid-1800s. They later took the Manitoba government up on land grants and settled east of the Cypress River.

They tended to be short in stature and when they formed an entire baseball team that travelled to North Dakota and beat a semi-pro team from Minot, they borrowed a taller player to cover first base.

The Youngs had an unfortunate history of fires burning down their homesteads. One great-grandmother was seriously burned in a house fire. One family had two farm homes burn down on separate occasions.

Percy Young, Neil Young's grandfather, became a pharmacist in nearby Glenboro until the Great Depression put him out of business. "He lost the store in 1930 because he couldn't turn down anyone with a sick kid," said his daughter, Liss. He opened a pharmacy in fledgling mining town Flin Flon in 1931, and the family didn't follow until 1937, she said.

The original Young brothers were very musical, as well as great step dancers. One of the original Young men was a great tenor. They set up big choirs, and someone later started an orchestra.

All the Youngs in Cypress River are related. "When I got married, I was the 13th Mrs. Young in Cypress River, and that was 55 years ago," said Marjorie Young, 78, who still lives there and is married to Walter Young.

Neil would visit as a child with his dad and stay at a farm owned by Garth and Dorothy Young, who are related through the singer's great-grandfather, John Young. "They would often stay with us on summer holidays," either driving or flying out from Ontario, Dorothy Young said. The last time he visited their farm was when he was eight or nine years old. Neil did not move from Ontario to Winnipeg until he was 14, after his parents divorced.

One new song, aptly titled *Far From Home*, relates a typical scene of the Young family making music. "My Uncle Bob sat at the piano, My girl cousins sang harmony, Those were the good old family times, That left a big mark on me."

Uncle Bob was her and Scott's brother, explained Liss. Bob often sat at the piano and started singalongs.

"My brother, Bob, was really musical, and he played by ear, and he played all the black notes because he had very fat fingers and couldn't get them between the black notes," said Liss. "He played and wrote a lot of songs in minor key."

Today, two local women descended from the Youngs are part of a band called Country Blend that plays country gospel in small Prairie towns.

Liss remembers how worry spread through the Young clan when Neil contracted polio as a child. He was in hospital in Toronto, and his condition wasn't improving. His parents took him to Florida so Neil could play in the warm waters there, and he finally started to get better.

"He was a fighter," she said of her nephew. "He always had something going on. He used to sell bait to the fishermen in Pickering [in Ontario, where he grew up]. And he had a garden and would sell vegetables at the roadside."

The famous musician has a namesake in Cypress River in Neil Young, who is employed by the Rural Municipality of Victoria in public works. Their names are merely a coincidence. Neil is 45, while his famous cousin is 60.

Neil and Debra Young and their three kids live in the last original Young home, a two-storey stone house built by great-grandfather William Edwin

Young in 1900. The children are the fifth generation of Youngs to live there.

Their Victorian-style stone house has been named a heritage building. It's constructed of granite boulders taken from the Assiniboine River and hauled 10 kilometres by horse-drawn stoneboat, a task of nearly Stonehenge-like proportions.

"They didn't have front-end loaders to lift it. They likely used scaffolds and a block-and-tackle system," said Neil. Even the basement was dug out so it could have a granite foundation. There is also a round, stone cistern in the basement. Water from the eaves funnelled into the cistern, and was then drawn up by a hand-pump.

It took more than a year to build the 1,400-square-foot house.

"It's an art to figure where to hit the boulder with the chisel to get the straight edges," said Neil. "I saw someone do it once. He'd walk around the rock, studying it, then set his chisel and give it a whack with a hammer."

Because the walls are made from granite blocks about 0.6 metres wide, the house has very wide window wells — wide enough to serve as mantles. Advantages to the granite blocks is they last forever, and you never have to paint them, Neil said.

Inside, there's a stamped tin ceiling, wainscotting along the kitchen walls, and original ruby red Battleship Linoleum. "It's what they put in the battleships in the war years because it was so tough," explained Neil.

He sought heritage status to protect the house after he's gone. "Our concern was if we sold, someone could just bulldoze the building."

The homestead of his famous cousin's great-grandfather was a mile to the east. All that's left there now is the cement foundation of the barn.

Whenever Neil plays in Winnipeg, there's a private party for the close cousins backstage.

His cousin's new CD sits on top of a stack of CDs. On the cover is a sepia-toned photograph of a woman hanging laundry on a clothesline in a gale.

"Just the farmer's wife hangin' laundry in her backyard, Out on the Prairie where the winds blow long and hard," Young sings.

It so happens a brightly coloured blanket is hanging desperately on the clothesline in the yard of the less famous Neil Young's stone house, too, in the face of a brisk wind.

When this coincidence is mentioned, Neil doesn't react much. One gets the impression wind is a constant here.

REAL LIFE IS AS RAUCOUS AS THE MOVIE
January 16, 2005

I wrote the following story during the 2004–2005 NHL work stoppage. People needed a hockey fix, including me. Spending an afternoon with Terry Marshall of Rapid City was just the antidote. Marshall was one of the hockey-playing extras from the Eastern Hockey League in the movie, Slapshot.

RAPID CITY — Terry Marshall remembered a real-life brawl between the Syracuse Blazers and the New York Long Island Ducks in the Eastern Hockey League, and the mayhem that followed.

Movie extra, Terry Marshall

"We had a trainer's table and a couple other things pushed against our dressing room door because the fans were using these long benches as battering rams to get at us," recalled Marshall, who played for the Blazers.

Police had to use security dogs to clear the arena, then told players to lie on the floor of the team bus as state troopers escorted the bus down the highway. They were worried someone might take a real-to-goodness pot shot at the players.

That was just one incident from the raucous Eastern Hockey League that inspired the movie classic *Slapshot*. Marshall, 55, was not only a hockey-playing extra in *Slapshot*, he lived much of the movie as an EHLer.

Slapshot, released in 1977, is today regarded as the *Gone With the Wind* of hockey movies. In this year of the Great Hockey Famine, many hockey fans need a lifeline to get them through winter, so Marshall agreed to reminisce about his experiences filming *Slapshot*.

He was interviewed from his horse ranch near Rapid City, just north of Brandon and 230 kilometres west of Winnipeg.

Mitchell's highlight reel of memories includes the antics of the Hanson Brothers (a.k.a. Jeff, Jack and Steve Carlson), the steady flow of booze courtesy of Universal Studios, and Paul Newman sitting in the dressing room, laughing as minor league tough guys swapped stories.

"He'd just sit there and shake his head, and say, 'I don't believe you guys," said Marshall.

Marshall, a seventh-round draft pick (92nd overall) in 1971 by the St. Louis Blues of the National Hockey League, toiled for five seasons as a rugged defensive defenceman in the EHL.

The now-defunct league was rodeo on skates. Mitchell rarely finished a game in the first half of his first year, due to injury or being thrown out for fighting. He describes his old Syracuse Blazers team as "two goal scor-ers and 15 protectors." Fights would break out during the warm-up skate. "You had to keep establishing yourself so nobody would run you."

It was not uncommon for players to take "bennies" — amphetamines that give a person more pep — and trainers were often the ones supplying them. Marshall wasn't among the users, but a defence partner, who went on to coach in the NHL, used to take two bennies before every game.

The Carlson brothers portrayed the Hanson brothers in the movie, sporting black-rimmed Buddy Holly glasses and creating chaos on the ice.

Mitchell remembers bashing heads many times in games with the Carlson brothers, who all played on the same line together. "If you hit one of them, the other two would come after you," Mitchell says.

The Carlson brothers really did get into a brawl in the stands in a game in Utica, N.Y., and were arrested, as depicted in the movie. The Carlsons also mooned opposing fans from their team bus, just like in the movie.

And a team from the EHL, later called North American Hockey League, really did fold because the tax loss was worth more to the owner than the sale price, which is the main plot of *Slapshot*. That team was the Long Island Ducks.

One tough guy Marshall fought regularly in real life was Ned Dowd of the Johnstown Jets.

"He came to me before one game and asked me if I'd like to be in a movie. I said he should tell me another one. He said he wanted to meet me in the bar after the game."

It turned out that Dowd's sister, Nancy Dowd, was a writer of several documentary films. She had tried her hand at writing a screenplay about the EHL, called *Slapshot*. Her brother helped her by recording dressing room banter with a tape recorder.

Universal Studios bought the script, and George Roy Hill, the Oscar-winning director with a penchant for buddy movies like *The Sting* and *Butch Cassidy and the Sundance Kid*, signed on to direct. Hill enlisted his friend, Newman.

Ned Dowd then rounded up about 30 EHL tough guys as extras, including Mitchell. He also summoned Connie "Mad Dog" Madigan, who was banned from hockey for hitting a referee over the head with his stick. CBC hockey commentator Don Cherry calls Madigan the toughest fighter he ever saw.

The move was a surprise hit, although it came under attack for its abundant profanity.

Later, Ned Dowd parlayed the experience into a career in Hollywood as a head of production and assistant director on dozens of movies, including *Hoffa*, *G.I. Jane*, and *Grosse Pointe Blank*. He was also executive producer of *Veronica Guerin*, starring Cate Blanchett. His sister, Nancy, became a comedy writer on television show *Saturday Night Live* for several years, and assisted with screenwriting on Oscar winners like *Ordinary People* and *Coming Home*. She sometimes works under pseudonyms Ernest Morton or Rob Morton.

Director George Roy Hill died in 2002. Paul Newman, an icon, who won a much-deserved best actor Oscar in Martin Scorsese's *The Color of Money* (1988), died in 2008.

Terry Marshall, who is originally from Virden and who played junior hockey for the Brandon Wheat Kings, doesn't have any speaking parts in *Slapshot*. He's the guy in the movie with the big black beard. He's in one early hockey scene, and appears again late in the movie as a member of the Syracuse team holding open a door, while Paul Newman and fictional hockey goon Dr. Hook jaw at each other.

It was a three-week party for the movie extras, said Marshall. Most of the time was spent sitting around drinking beer. They'd have to be dressed in their hockey gear by 7 a.m., but usually wouldn't get called to skate until late afternoon. Their scenes basically involved chasing the puck into the corner and crashing into each other. One time, a real fight started and turned into a brawl. The camera crew filmed it all, then asked them to do a retake.

"Universal Studios treated us A-1 all the way," said Marshall.

The closest Marshall came to making it to the big leagues was when he was called up for two games with the New York Blades of the defunct World Hockey Association. The gimmick with the Blades was that players had to wear white skates.

Mitchell got on for five shifts. His career highlight came against the Houston Aeros. He went into a corner with none other than Mr. Hockey, Gordie Howe, who was then 54 years of age. Howe had a way of saying hello with his elbows.

"We went into a corner and I felt this whoosh, his elbow just brushing my nose," he said. He ended up playing with Howe years later in an oldtimers' game.

After five seasons, injuries to Marshall's knees convinced him to seek another career.

Today, Marshall buys and sells horses, and has won many awards on the rodeo circuit. He also runs M2 Ranch Hay Rides in Brandon, and is a cattle inspector with the Saskatchewan government.

ONE SICK DAY IN 61 YEARS
October 12, 2004

STE. ANNE — So how many times has Alice Langill called in sick in her 61 years as church organist for the Ste. Anne des Chenes Catholic Church, playing up to three services per Sunday?

Once.

Alice Langill in Ste. Anne des Chenes Catholic Church

"I had the flu," laughs Langill, 87, looking almost embarrassed by her astonishing attendance record.

"She's reliable," said Father Ren Chartier, which is a bit like saying the *Titanic* had a fender-bender.

But when it was suggested to Father Chartier that a certain someone may already have secured a ticket to heaven, he cautioned that's not for mere mortals to say.

"That's not my department," he said. However, he added, "she's fulfilling a wonderful service I'm sure the Lord will not ignore."

Langill doesn't play just any organ but the oldest pipe organ in the province, built in 1923. Nuns entreated her to take over as organist because she didn't have any children and "I had time." Langill, who was 25 at the time and married, refused at first.

"They started in April after me, and I said no, no, no. Finally they said you have to."

She began in July, 1943. A nun gave her a crash course in how to play the pipe organ in four lessons. Langill had some piano training but hadn't touched a keyboard in 10 years.

She has also played at more than 1,000 funerals, and hundreds of weddings.

Langill rarely even takes a holiday. She hasn't had a real vacation in about two decades, since her husband Stephen, a carpenter, passed away.

The town of Ste. Anne, 60 kilometres east of Winnipeg, is delighted that such a humble, previously unsung hero as Langill is getting some attention. Parties were thrown and gifts presented to her on her 25th and 50th anniversaries as church organist.

"Her playing is magnificent, especially when she plays 'Panis Anjelicus'. We cannot do without Alice, I'll tell you," said Denise Henzel, a member of the church choir

"She's a great lady. She says, 'I'm easily replaced.' I said, 'No you're not, Alice,'" Henzel said.

"This is her way of serving the Lord in this community. She does this from the goodness of her heart," said Father Chartier.

Langill said her enthusiasm for playing has been renewed by the church's new European-trained choir director Erika Wihrly. "I'm still interested in doing it, but it's getting harder for me," she said, holding up a hand to reveal the onset of arthritis. Langill's favourite hymns are "How Great Thou Art", and "Fill My House". Her favourite Christmas carol is "Holy Night".

People dressed a lot differently for church when she started — women in long sleeves and hats, men in white shirts and black suits.

"When I started, high mass was in Latin," she recalled. "In the 1950s, it changed to French. And a few years later, there were more English people, and it started English mass, too."

She played all three services, about 10 hymns per service — early morning low mass, late morning high mass, and afternoon vespers. She lived about a kilometre away, and would walk to church and back each time because she and her husband didn't own a vehicle. When they bought an old truck a decade later, she still had to walk in winter because the truck couldn't run in the cold.

Langill has outlasted nine choir directors, and numerous priests.

Although she originally received a modest fee for her playing, she now volunteers her time.

"At first, I got $10 a month, then it went to $12, and every three or four years it would go up. I was up to $1,000 a year, at $90 a month."

But then she stopped accepting payment. "I told them because the choir wasn't paid, why should I be paid?"

She has had people suggest to her that she is being taken advantage of.

"I say no, no. They need me... It's something you can give to the church," she said.

"It's my life. I have no children," she said. "I get lots of thank-yous, and people are really nice to me."

Langill is a retired seamstress at the Villa Youville seniors residence in Ste. Anne.

THE SAGE IN AUGUST
September 28, 2008

BRANDON — He's got stories.

Oh man, does Fred McGuinness have stories.

There's the story about his first job as a CPR telegraph operator at age 15, and how he thought he'd found his true love in an unseen operator in another prairie town.

Former *Brandon Sun* executive and editor Fred McGuinness

McGuinness got to know the other operator while working evenings. He'd clacked away sweet nothings to that person, who went by the name Brenda, trying to arrange a tryst. That is, until he discovered it was another male operator putting him on.

"He kept me going for six months," said McGuinness. "I was totally deflated when I found out."

You want a sign-of-the-times story? McGuinness tells of standing in a grocery store checkout line recently when a cellphone rang and the whole lineup of people started fishing through purses and pockets to see if it was their phone.

Then there are his stories about chauffeuring Tommy Douglas around rural Saskatchewan in the mid-1950s, when that province was celebrating its 50th anniversary. Douglas was premier of Saskatchewan at the time and introduced health care in Canada.

"The wit, and caring, and strength of personality of that man. He was almost impossible to believe," McGuinness says admiringly. But listening to Douglas's jokes was torture. "He'd get up before an audience and say, 'A couple from Broadview that I know moved out to the West Coast and he took up golf and she took up going to auctions. And once in awhile he will wake up in the middle of the night and yell, 'Fore!' and she will wake up and yell, 'Four and a half!'"

"He had unbelievable corn," said McGuinness.

At age 87, legendary newspaperman and author McGuinness is still telling stories.

He's been writing for newspapers for more than half a century, since he broke in with the *Medicine Hat News* in 1955. He joined the *Brandon Sun* in 1966 — he was born in Brandon — and still writes a weekly column 43 years later. "He's got legions of readers, that guy," said *Brandon Sun* managing editor James O'Connor.

While at the *Brandon Sun*, McGuinness also wrote for *Reader's Digest* for a dozen years. He hosted the former CBC weekly show, *Neighbourly News*, for about 10 years until its cancellation in 1987. *Neighbourly News* was broadcast at 8:30 every Sunday morning for 44 years.

After that, McGuinness syndicated a *Neighbourly News* newspaper column that ran in rural weeklies across the prairies. Problems with his eyesight forced him to stop in 2001.

Over the course of his career, he became what sounds like an oxymoron today — a famous rural media personality. He helped bridge the chasm between "the hicks and the slicks," as he put it — rural and urban people, in case you didn't guess.

He's written about a dozen books, including *Manitoba: The Province and the People*, for which he won the Margaret McWilliams Medal for best Manitoba history book.

He also wrote prairie essays for 17 years for CBC Radio's *Morningside* with Peter Gzowski, some of which were put in book form in *Letters from Section 17* (Great Plains Publications). Gzowski once called McGuinness "the master of the anecdote."

Today, at his age, "it's anecdotage," cracked McGuinness.

"Look for an old geezer with the walking stick and a hearing aid," he said over the phone, when it was arranged to meet at the Victoria Inn restaurant in Brandon.

He calls his infirmities, "my impairities." "I can't see, I can't hear, and I can't walk," he groused. But he can write. He can't stop. "I'm a compulsive writer," he said.

He reads on the computer — and he still reads a lot — by jacking the font to about six times the print size you're reading now. He has macular degeneration: the loss of vision in the centre of the visual field.

As for his hearing, it got so that every diner in the restaurant probably heard the reporter's overly-loud, oft-repeated questions.

"Do you get a lot of e-mail?" he is asked at one point, on the subject of reader reaction.

"Oh, yeah. Quite heavily female."

"No, e-mail. On the computer."

McGuinness laughed. "Both. I bet it's been a long time since you've had a letter in the mail in a hand-written envelope. I still get them and a lot of people just leave them on the desk of the *Brandon Sun*."

"The Voice of the Prairies," as he was called when he received the Order of Canada in 2004, is now "just old Fred," he claims.

Don't believe it. He's called far worse on occasion.

Like when he waded into the recent controversy over abortion activist Henry Morgentaler being awarded the Order of Canada. McGuinness, to the surprise of many, publicly applauded the decision. He grew up the only male in a household of women and absorbed many of their feminist views, he explained.

Readers gave McGuinness a tongue-lashing. Brandon has one of the highest concentrations of evangelical Christians, according to the Canada census. McGuinness was even yelled at in a coffee shop.

McGuinness smiles impishly about it. He's an old newspaper man and, to him, that's like getting a pat on the back.

"That's OK," he says. "I want a reaction and I get it."

Not that he would say something just to get a rise from people. It's more difficult to be outspoken in a small community than in a large urban centre.

But with McGuinness, one gets the impression that even the most heated arguments are just a mispronunciation or verbal slip away from turning into a belly laugh and a handshake.

"He is just a fine, fine gentleman, a real people person," said Jim Lewthwaite, *Brandon Sun* city editor. "Even now, he's still sharp and will come into the newsroom at least once a week and give me a news tip or a tune-up [on journalism]."

McGuinness learned to be the man of the house early. His father died when Fred was 12 and "it was as if a light had gone out in my life," he told University of Manitoba historian Gerald Friesen, in a 1981 interview for the Manitoba Historical Society.

He was the only boy in a household of seven women: his widowed mother, five sisters, and a maid. "I was raised in a Protestant nunnery," he jokes.

A maid? "A maid in those days was a country girl whose family can't afford to feed her... Brandon had a maid in just about every household," he explained.

He felt lost without his father and couldn't focus on school. He scraped through Grade 7 but it took him two years to pass Grade 8. He failed Grade 9 and quit school, taking the telegraph job in Brandon.

He joined the navy at 18 when the Second World War broke out in 1939. He was injured and spent a year in the hospital in a body brace. He needed two canes to learn to walk again. He attended old St. Paul's High College in Winnipeg and graduated.

It was in 1942–43, while studying pre-med at University of Manitoba, that his life took a detour that eventually landed him in journalism.

Another story. "The first day I was handed a note to go to the office of the dean. I thought, 'What's this?' He wanted me to be a speaker for the war finance committee to promote war bonds."

McGuinness was chosen partly because of his war experience and his visible injury, but also for his commanding voice. He initially wanted no part of the dean's plan but at $8 a speech, well, no one said Fred

McGuinness ever refused a chance to make a buck.

He gave speeches in aircraft factories, Winnipeg downtown offices, and the grain pit of the Winnipeg Grain Exchange.

He also realized the field of medicine wasn't for him. He got a job with the federal government as a speechwriter. The Saskatchewan government began looking for a writer who was also a good public speaker, to run its 50th anniversary.

Writers tend to be poor public speakers. The Saskatchewan government couldn't find a single candidate in its province. It was McGuinness's war bonds experience that got him the job.

That's how he got to know Tommy Douglas. Later, as the term position neared its end in 1955, the *Medicine Hat News* offered McGuinness a writing job. He was on his way to being a journalist. "The matter of public speaking made the difference," he maintains.

Oratory and writing have always gone hand in hand for McGuinness. Many former journalism students in Manitoba will remember McGuinness as a guest speaker. Many will also remember his dictum: "There's no such thing as a boring story, only boring storytellers." Be interesting!

"The thing noticeable about Fred is his absolutely distinctive voice and manner of speaking. He was stopped many times in airports because people had heard him on Peter Gzowski and recognized him by his voice," said Tom Mitchell, Brandon University head of archives.

His columns today are different from most others. A McGuinness column can change subjects rapidly, and leap-frog from one lily pad to the next, each paragraph representing a new subject.

One column began about waking at 3:15 a.m. and "having to go down the hall. If, on your way back to bed you say to yourself, 'I think I'll check my e-mail,' then it is confirmed: you are an electronic addict." From there, he covered text messaging, pointless cell phone calls, the Canadian Wheat Board, the Royal Winter Fair, and memoir writing, which he still teaches, all in 600 words.

A McGuinness column is always open to anecdotal interruptions from life. One column started describing an archaeology dig in southwestern

Manitoba. But halfway through the column, after having visited the dig site, Fred wrote that he found himself covered in wood ticks.

He removed 19 of them and thought that was all, but two days later discovered a tick "the size of a small blueberry" nestled in his navel. This reminded him about the son of a publisher of the *Carman Valley Leader* who went on a camping trip, felt something peculiar inside his pajama, and groped in the moonlight in search of a flashlight. He found a woodtick "attempting to get into that tiny opening in the head of the penis."

It was vintage Fred McGuinness — a story about archaeology sidetracked by woodticks and their fondness for male pudenda.

Asked if he ever contemplated starting a blog [online journal], McGuinness says he has, if only to rail against Prime Minister Stephen Harper.

With that statement he breaks old pal Gzowski's motto to never let the audience know where you stand on issues. McGuinness believes that's also the key to success for long-time CNN television talk host, Larry King.

But it's too late for McGuinness to start muzzling his opinions. He views Harper as a Reform Party holdover in sheep's clothing. McGuinness bristles at Harper's vendetta against the Canadian Wheat Board. It took the courts to force Harper's government to stop.

"[Harper] views the Canadian Wheat Board as socialism. But I tell you it was people working together that settled these prairies," McGuinness said.

On the Liberals, he wished the party had put out a "Dick and Jane reader" on its carbon tax proposal long ago.

The anti-Harper talk seems strange considering McGuinness resides in Conservative Party heartland. Brandon is solidly Conservative, except for East Brandon, which votes NDP provincially. Rural southwestern Manitoba elects Tories sight unseen.

So how does that jive with McGuinness being a major voice for prairie people?

McGuinness doesn't pander to his audience, said Lewthwaite, who edits McGuinness's column. "You sometimes think of these small daily columnists who are pretty right wing and you can tell they're playing to their constituency. Fred's just not like that. He rises above the pettiness of that," Lewthwaite said.

"He loves to tweak noses," said Lewthwaite. But he doesn't offend. "He takes his hardest shots at public figures, without demeaning people who believe in those public figures."

Even so, McGuinness is not a political writer. He writes "more on life and times, than on politics," Lewthwaite said.

McGuinness doesn't disagree. "I get so mad at young journalists who think writing about politics is everything."

One McGuinness trait is always wanting to know where people are from. "He calls me 'The Pride of Deloraine' because I'm originally from Deloraine," said Lewthwaite. "And he will latch on to that and any news tip or any information about Deloraine he will make sure I know about it."

Fred and his wife Christine live on a 32-acre parcel of land just west of Brandon. It was intended to be a Christmas tree farm but when the time came they couldn't bring themselves to cut them down.

Even at the age of 87, McGuinness cannot stand to be idle. He can go on and on about the great waste of human resources when people spend gobs of time in front of the television.

Don't get him started on the media's treatment of rural Canada either. "We've come to a transition in which the cities are the focus of media attention, and rural society is pretty much forgotten," he maintained.

He has met and known the likes of Tommy Douglas, John Diefenbaker, and Queen Elizabeth II but they aren't necessarily his favourite interviews. "Fred finds characters more interesting than famous people," said Mitchell.

"His interests are without limit, particularly when it comes to rural Canada. He's a natural-born journalist down to his toenails," Mitchell said.

"I greatly admire the man," said Lewthwaite. "He's always got a twinkle in his eye. He really has a marvellous sense of humour."

Said Lewthwaite: "He has keen interest in everything still. He's still offering news tips and editing tips. He's never lost that."

FRED MCGUINNESS TIMELINE

- Fred McGuinness was born in Brandon on January 31, 1921.
- Quit school in Grade 9 and worked as CPR telegraph operator
- Enlisted in the navy in 1939 during the Second World War. Attended St. Paul's College on his return.
- Worked on Saskatchewan's Golden Jubilee from 1952 to 1955.
- From 1955–65, he wrote for the *Medicine Hat News*, and became vice-president and publisher.
- From 1966 until the present, he has written for the *Brandon Sun* and served as vice-president and publisher.
- Received the Order of Manitoba in 2002, and an honorary law degree from Brandon University.
- Received the Order of Canada in 2004.

Some Fred McGuinness anecdotes:

- On former CBC Radio host Peter Gzowski: "I'll tell you something that Gzowski did that no one else every did. He introduced you to a whole bunch of little towns and interesting people in little towns, and he got away from Toronto and Montreal and Vancouver. He became the king of rural life, as far as I was concerned."

- On meeting Queen Elizabeth II (McGuinness was part of the committee that planned her visit): "When she found out I was a beekeeper, she just took me over to a table and we had a private chat because she was a beekeeper. The other [committee members] couldn't believe it. She wanted to know if I had any seven-banded Italian honey bees."

- McGuinness once wrote of a woman in Hudson Bay, Saskatchewan (near the Manitoba border) who was celebrating her 73rd wedding anniversary. He asked her why, in these modern times, she never divorced. "She said it was funny he should mention it. She said, 'I never, ever thought of divorce. Mind you, I often thought of murder.'"

- On former Progressive Conservative Prime Minister John Diefenbaker, whom McGuinness got to know as a backbencher: "When he got up in the House of Commons, his forefinger seemed to stretch about three feet long, when he pointed it at the opposition Liberals," said McGuinness. "I thought he was a warm, warm person and I couldn't vote for him because he was so erratic."

We lost this great "Voice of the Prairies" in March, 2011. It was an honour and privilege to sit down and talk with Fred. We kept in touch by phone and email afterward, as I know he did with many people.

MÉTIS MAN STORMED BEACHES ON D-DAY
June 7, 2002

BOISSEVAIN — At age six, Frank Godon lived in a shack with an earth floor.

At age 12, he left his Métis family to plow and harrow white farmers' fields. At age 16, he drove a truck delivering ice and coal.

And on D-Day — June 6, 1944 — Godon stormed the beaches of Normandy as an anti-tank gunner for Canada.

The sea was red. Bullets sounded, bullets thudded into arms and legs and torsos, men screamed. Godon ran up the beach, zigzagging to avoid enemy fire. "You saw your friends go down and you couldn't stop," he said.

Can we imagine it? No. Should we at least try? Yes.

Yesterday marked the anniversary of that pivotal Second World War battle that gave Allied forces a foothold in Europe versus Hitler-led Germany. Within 11 months, the Allied forces routed Hitler.

As he recalls Normandy, Godon's voice is a raspy whisper, a souvenir from his days as a prisoner of war. He was captured on the third day of the invasion. Because Germany didn't have enough soldiers to look after

Second World War vet Frank Godon

POWs, it placed prisoners like Godon in concentration camps.

Gestapo guards beat Godon with rifle butts about the head and throat more than once. He lost most of his voice, is blind in one eye, and one side of his face is paralysed.

"Those people who say there were no Jews? I was there. I saw them," he said.

Yet there's something strangely charmed about Godon's life. He was witness to some of the worst atrocities the 20th century had to offer — D-Day, concentration camps, racism against people of aboriginal descent — and not only survived but prospered.

Godon had no formal education. Godon went to school twice — once for two months, and later for a month and a half. Yet he would practise reading and writing on his own. After the war, he launched a highly successful manufacturing business — Godon Industries — in Boissevain with his brother.

Godon also fought, and fought often, anyone who called him names like half-breed or worse. "I once fought seven times the same night. I had no shirt left. But you don't have to put that in the paper," he said.

Much later, Godon rode around Winnipeg in a limousine when his nephew, Yvon Dumont, was named Manitoba's lieutenant governor.

Godon, now 78, was raised in the Métis community of Lake Metigoshe in the Turtle Mountains in southwestern Manitoba, where his father farmed a quarter section.

"I'll say this for my father. He never once was on relief," Godon said.

Not a teenager yet, Godon worked 12-hour days doing man's work in farmers' fields. He enlisted at 17, lying about his age. The army rejected him four times due to his lack of education, before accepting him. "I told them, 'Just give me a chance. We want to win this war'."

He trained in Canada, and became a Royal Winnipeg Rifle, and was shipped to England. His unit received special intensive training for two months but wasn't told why. "We knew something was going on but we didn't know what."

Finally, they were shipped out. He would be among the first wave of Canadian soldiers to land on Juno Beach. "The commanding officer said, 'I'm going to tell you guys. None of you guys are coming home'," Godon recalled.

The job of the anti-tank platoon was to draw enemy fire and push the Germans back so Allied tanks and equipment could land on the beach. Godon still has nightmares about the event, and said agreeing to be interviewed brought on a recent nightmare.

"Your buddies were falling. You couldn't help them. They were yelling. Water's up to your neck. And you couldn't help them," he said.

He was part of the Third Canadian Division, Royal Winnipeg Rifles, B Company. His company entered the edge of Courseulles, called the "hot zone." But Allied bombers had missed their targets, so the Canadian men were left unprotected. Their landing craft were met with a hail of bullets.

"The beach was, you know, bodies and body pieces floating," he said.

Steel girders, rolls of barbed wire, and land mines were scattered across the beach to prevent such an invasion. "We were just getting on the beach. The Germans had been waiting for us for years," said Godon.

The estimated 120 men in Company B were cut down to one officer and

25 men in the first 12 hours.

They pushed back the Germans, but too quickly, and got cut off from their own tanks coming in behind. They were soon surrounded by Germans. Companies A, B and C had lost so many men they teamed together. They surrendered on June 8.

But it was who they surrendered to that spelled the end for many of the Canadians. It was the German 12th SS division. From the Winnipeg Rifles, 58 soldiers who surrendered were shot dead on the spot. In total, 156 Canadian soldiers were murdered by the SS.

Again, Godon somehow survived. He and the remaining prisoners marched for the next 18 days. They slept in small-town cemeteries because they were fenced. In July, Godon and about 40 men spent 28 days in a hot boxcar being shuffled between concentration camps. Raw sewage covered the floor. Their rations were "a few ounces of bread and slop."

He was placed in more than one concentration camp. "Prisoners would die every day," he said. "You'd go to the washroom and there'd be someone dead because they died of diarrhea."

When Victory in Europe Day arrived on May 8, 1945, American soldiers freed Godon and his fellow prisoners. "The Americans treated us like kings," he said. But when he was handed over to Canadian authorities a week later, it was a different story. Fearing some of the soldiers might be Germans in disguise, the men were put into a barbed-wire barracks as if they were prisoners again.

Godon entered the army weighing 205 pounds. He came back weighing just over 90 pounds.

Godon is not sure why he's survived so many brushes with death. He's an incredibly strong man, but he feels he's been kept alive for some reason he can't fathom.

For example, when captured by Germans and made to march, an Allied plane strafed the men with bullets. The prisoners on either side of Godon were hit and killed, but he survived.

Another example: While he and prisoners were being moved in a boxcar, an Allied plane took out the railroad bridge minutes after their train crossed it. Even the ship which delivered Godon to England had its stern bombed out by German planes hours after he and his fellow troops disembarked.

Godon had triple bypass heart surgery a few years ago but went into the bush last winter and still cut and split eight cords of birch wood. He's the oldest active trapper in the Turtle Mountains.

The licence plate on his car reads: POW-WW2. The plate on his truck reads the reverse: WW2-POW.

He explains: "We went over there. Lots of us boys never came back. So I felt I had to make people realize we were the boys who went over there to conquer Hitler."

PRAIRIE PROLIFERATION
March 16, 2010

MORDEN — Raising 14 children doesn't seem so unusual to parents Eduard and Alla Schlak.

After all, Eduard came from a family of seven children, Alla from a family of 11.

Five of Alla's brothers have more than 10 children.

As for grandchildren? Take a deep breath: Alla's mother has 107 grandchildren.

"When Alla's mother prays, she mentions every grandchild and she remembers every grandchild's name," said Florian, 18, the Schlak family's eldest son.

Rural depopulation? Not here. Not since the

Family of Eduard and Alla Schlak of Morden

Manitoba Nominee Program that matches immigrants with job-skill shortages in Manitoba began in the late 1990s.

The Schlak family, loosely called Russian Germans because they first emigrated from Russia and then from Germany, are part of the population growth in the Pembina Valley that has shot through the roof. The RM of Stanley, which surrounds Winkler and Morden, has seen its population jump 55 per cent since 2000.

Brandon is also seeing a boom in Latin American immigrants who settle after arriving on work visas with the Maple Leaf Foods plant. The Wheat City's population has increased 17 per cent since 2000. There are up to a dozen other pockets of significant immigration growth in rural Manitoba.

"It's a stunning story. Immigration has breathed new life into a host of communities," said Joseph Warbanski, head economic statistician with the Manitoba Bureau of Statistics.

But it's an old story, too. What about the Schlaks? What's it like to raise 14 kids?

It's like the year 1910.

The respect level between children and parents in the Schlak family is very *Little House on the Prairie*. You half expect the children to address their parents as Ma or Pa, like Laura Ingalls in the popular book and 1974-83 TV series.

Discipline is maintained in a kind of trickle-down system, from parents to eldest, eldest to next eldest, and so on down the line. It's noteworthy how responsible the oldest children are in caring for the littlest ones.

The Schlaks also have two cats, two dogs, 33 chickens, "and one chicken husband," said Eduard. (This is a family in-joke, repeating what a Russian they met in the United States called a rooster.) They produce as much food as they can and have a storage room full of jarred preserves like beets and jams.

When family members take the bus to school, they fill half the seats. Eight children take the bus.

The family has no TV. "We have 14 channels we have to watch," said

Eduard, meaning his children.

"We are our own entertainment," added Florian.

That explains why there are almost as many musical instruments in the house as children: a trumpet, tuba, euphonium, two electric pianos, violins, a double bass, accordion and pan flutes. The parents can only afford introductory music lessons but the children continue to learn on their own.

They have one shower and two toilets. "If we all get up at the same time, there's a lineup," said Florian. But usually it's manageable. That may change when the family's six girls, all 10 and under now, begin to mature. (Just saying!) There's also an outhouse for summer use.

Alla says she gets lots of help managing the house. The children take turns to do the chores, including cooking, washing dishes, cleaning the house, and reading a passage from the Bible at the end of the day. Mom does a major house cleaning once a month. Everyone goes to bed about 9 p.m.

Eduard and Alla can't transport the whole family very easily. They have an SUV and a truck but it still takes two trips to go anywhere. They rarely go out all together.

For example, although the family is very devout, the smallest children stay home from church on Sundays and an older sibling babysits. Like two generations ago when families were also large, the church is the centre of the family's life.

Even though the boys never played organized soccer in Germany, the three oldest were recruited to the Morden Collegiate team because all Germans are supposed to be good at soccer. With 13 Germans and five Canadians, the Morden squad bested rival teams in Winkler and Portage la Prairie and went all the way to the provincials, finishing fourth in 2009.

The Schlaks live in a 1,300-square-foot bungalow. That works out to about 80 square feet per person. Everyone learns how to be alone in a crowd. At one point, two of the older sons were found seated in the basement in the dark listening to music, just getting away from the hubbub.

When the weather warms up, there's plenty of room on their 11-acre lot just west of Morden.

Although they have no TV, the family does have two computers. School work gets priority, and the computers are not used for gaming.

The family eats in shifts, the smaller ones taking meals first right after school. The parents could not say what the monthly food bill comes out to.

They don't scrimp on food. For supper, Alla served something called gyros, a delicious Greek soup that included paprika, rice, chicken, corn, mushrooms, potatoes and onions. Then there was a Russian dish called *monty*, which might be called *fleisch perishke* in many Ukrainian or Mennonite homes in Manitoba, but bigger and with a denser dough. There was also something called *schuba*, a kind of quiche casserole of pork, green onions, carrots and eggs compacted in a big pie dish with a topping of shredded beets. (*Schuba* means "in a fur coat" in Russian and the Internet calls it a salad.)

For dessert, Alla served a pink cream-cheese cake and something the family called *kulbassa* — a sweet chocolate roll the colour and texture of an Eat More candy bar, sliced like sausage.

Florian, who speaks English very well, interprets for his parents, who only speak Russian and German. Florian is also called upon to take and make phone calls on behalf of the family. He will work to help support the family once he completes high school this year.

There are five bedrooms, one of them a converted attached garage that also serves as a playroom. One of the rooms sleeps four girls on a double bunk.

The family had trouble with its immigration papers and was almost sent back to Germany. Their confirmation of permanent residency was only approved in February 2011. Federal immigration officials questioned Eduard's ability to support such a large family and, despite his job at Decor Cabinets, were considering ordering the family back to Germany.

But the Manitoba government intervened, saying Eduard has valuable job skills as a certified carpenter. The Schlaks also have a large support system of family and friends here. They receive financial assistance from grandparents on both sides, and from fellow Christians of the Gospel Faith church.

"My dad says he's thankful for the government supporting us," said Florian.

The gender of the Schlak children follows a peculiar pattern. The first six children were boys: Florian (18); Dennis (17); Julian (15); Fabian (14); Jonathon (13); and Ilian (11). Then the girls took over: Miriam (10); Lilian (8); Vivian (4); Jilian (3); and twins Edith and Judith (2).

Sandwiched in between was a boy, Maximilian (7), and lastly, Jimmy, five months.

There could be more on the way. Mother and father are still relatively young. Eduard is 37 and Alla is 38. "It's up to God," said Alla.

That would mean more grandchildren to test the memory of Alla's mother, who lives in Germany. She's only 70.

WHO ARE RUSSIAN GERMANS?

THEY are Germans who were invited by Catherine the Great to settle open land in Russia in the late 18th century. The Russian empress particularly targeted German immigrants because of their reputation for farming and industry. Catherine the Great allowed newcomers to keep their language and religion and not be assimilated.

All that changed with the Russian Revolution and the ensuing communist dictatorships. Then-leader Mikhail Gorbachev unravelled the Soviet Union and the Russian Germans were free to leave. German Chancellor Helmut Kohl welcomed them back.

But they didn't feel at home. German people called them Russians and looked down on them for having large families. When businesswoman Adele Dyck of Winkler brought over the first Russian Germans in 1998, as part of a pilot project under the Gary Filmon government, it started a tidal wave of immigration to southern Manitoba.

ADAM BEACH'S EARLY YEARS
May 10, 2008

VOGAR — The irony is Sally Beach was feeling lucky that night.

It was about 10:30 on a rainy Thursday night, May 28, 1981. Sally had just won at bingo in nearby Lundar and was returning home with treats for her three boys.

Vogar is a Métis village near Lake Manitoba Narrows in the Interlake. Sally Beach is the late mother of Adam Beach, one of Canada's biggest TV and movie stars and an inspiration to aboriginal people.

Sally, 28, was eight months pregnant. She and husband, Dennis, already knew it was a girl to complement their three boys, Chris, 9, Adam, 8, and David, 6.

An aunt and uncle dropped her off on the gravel road across from her house. The house is still there. When back visiting family, Adam has been known to drop in and visit the house and walk into his old bedroom.

People always say Adam takes after his mother. Sally was one of those people who's like the sun shining on everyone, people who knew her say. She radiated a positive energy on whoever she met, aboriginal or members of the Icelandic community here. Those are the groups who predominate in the Lake Manitoba Narrows area. Sally was from the prominent Swan family in neighbouring Lake Manitoba First Nation, an Ojibway band.

"She'd come across the street all the time for coffee," said Bev Johnson, who taught Sally's three boys in the K-6 Vogar School. "You were always glad to see her. She always made you feel better."

Sally Beach, Adam Beach's mother

Marlene Swan, who married Sally's brother, Allan, sees so much of Sally in Adam. "That's the way his mom was, the way he moves around and the way he talks," said Marlene.

Sally was attractive, too. Combined with "a bubbly outgoing personality, the result is a most captivating individual," wrote W. John

Johnson, a farmer near Vogar who self-published his diaries in a book called *The 80s: Triumphs and Tragedies.*

She was ahead of her time, a "modern" aboriginal woman, Johnson wrote. Back then, many aboriginal women greeted you with "downcast eyes [that] failed to meet your own." But not Sally. "She talked to everyone on equal terms."

Chris Beach, 37, the oldest of Sally's boys, who now lives in Lake Manitoba First Nation next door to Vogar, remembers his mom always singing. She wasn't the least bit shy and sang at many Interlake dances. Sally also wrote songs, painted, and was a former Manitoba jigging champion. Entertaining was in her blood.

Donna Steinthorson, a nurse who administered to Sally at the accident scene that night, believes Sally could have been a professional singer. "I thought she could go somewhere because she was that good, and everybody recognized that. She would have liked to have done what Adam has done," Steinthorson said.

It will never be completely clear what happened next. Three teenagers were joyriding. The driver was a 16-year-old who lived two doors down from the Beaches. He was driving very fast, very recklessly on the wrong side of a residential gravel road.

It happened so suddenly, so unexpectedly. All she had to do was walk across the road. That's all. But she was pregnant and carrying groceries. The car struck Sally with such violence. She slammed into the windshield. The vehicle carried her 60 metres before she fell onto the shoulder.

The car never stopped. Sally never regained consciousness.

"The angels must have wept," Johnson wrote.

Husband Dennis, also 28, was Métis and a journeyman carpenter. His father, Christopher, was white, a mix of English and Icelandic, and his mother, Anne, was Ojibway.

Dennis was shattered by Sally's death. At her wake, he held onto the casket and begged her not to leave. He tried to drown his sorrow with alcohol.

"[Dad] was always drunk. He cried all the time, although he tried not to let us see it," said Chris, the oldest son.

Not two months later, on a hot July 11, Dennis and four friends went to a local swimming hole. It was a small gravel pit and not considered dangerous. They all swam across, and when the others turned around, Dennis was gone.

Adam Beach

It was as if someone had let tragedy out of a locked cellar and it stalked the countryside. How Dennis drowned is a matter of speculation. He was an excellent swimmer. Some people believe his death was suicide from a broken heart. He was also on medication for depression, a lethal mix with alcohol. Perhaps his drowning was a just slip-up when he had little will to live.

Within a span of 41 days, their three children, Chris, Adam and David Beach had become orphans.

* * *

If you type the name Adam Beach into Google, photos pop up of Adam at movie premieres, award shows, post-award parties, posing with other stars and starlets, in movie and TV stills.

The 35-year-old actor has starred in several top-flight movies since his breakthrough with the lead role in *Squanto: A Warrior's Tale* in 1994, including *Dance Me Outside, Smoke Signals, Windtalkers, Flags of Our Fathers* (directed by Clint Eastwood) and *Bury My Heart at Wounded Knee* on HBO, for which he was nominated for a Golden Globe.

He recently starred in the hit TV series *Law & Order: Special Victims Unit* as Chester Lake, a Mohawk investigator. Chester Lake was also a victim. One episode revealed that his character bounced around foster homes as a child.

That's not much different from Adam's real life following his parents' deaths.

The orphaned boys went to live in Winnipeg with their Aunt Donna, on their father's side. Five years later, they moved in with an uncle, Chris Beach, who became their legal guardian. Adam was 13 and Chris, 14. At 15, Adam moved again to live with his mom's sister, Alice and her husband Dan Roulette, also in Winnipeg. He moved out at about 18 and lived on his own.

People credit the extended Beach family with giving the boys a strong upbringing. One resident in the Narrows area described the Beaches as "very smart people," and another said, "no one in the Beach family is shy." Adam's father was one of 11 children who started out in Vogar, six of whom became teachers. Among the other three, one is a social worker, one a computer programmer, and Dennis was a journeyman carpenter.

How did Adam Beach become a famous actor?

Adam's oldest brother Chris, 36, lives in Lake Manitoba First Nation. You can tell right away Chris is Adam's brother. You might even think he's Adam. He is frequently mistaken for his famous brother and gets a lot of stares and requests for autographs. That applies doubly when he goes to the theatre to see one of his brother's movies.

Chris said Adam always told him he'd be famous. "He said, 'I'll pick you up in a limo and I'll have a big mansion.'"

It was apparent at an early age that Adam was especially gifted. He excelled at so many things, both scholastics and sports, and was always doing things to make money, like collect empty bottles for the deposit.

He was smart in school "and he could really talk," said Chris. He would come into higher grades to get books because he had read all the ones in his grade. Then he would read bedtime stories to his older cousins. Sally nicknamed him 'Book.'

"He was into everything on the reserve. Skateboarding, breakdancing. He was an extreme kid," said Jason Swan, who is Adam's uncle, but, at only two years older, more like a friend. When Adam became lonely shooting his first movie *Squanto*, he asked Jason to stay with him, and Jason did for five weeks.

One of the stories people tell about Adam is the time he wrote a note to his Grade 2 teacher, Esther Johnson. She had disciplined him and so the next day he put a note on her desk and went home: "I'm mad at you and I'm not coming to school today. Love, Adam."

It was the "Love, Adam" that always cracked her up. She kept the letter all her life, not knowing Adam would become famous one day. Before she died, she passed it on to her husband Conrad. When he was dying of cancer, he got the message out that Adam should visit him because he had something to give him. Adam came and read the note and laughed.

Acting became an all-consuming passion for Adam while attending Gordon Bell High School, but his grades suffered and that worried his guardian, Chris.

"I thought, 'What you're thinking is an impossibility,'" recalled Chris, his adoptive father, not to be confused with Adam's brother, Chris. "Number one, you're from the North End. Number two, you're aboriginal. What chance do you have to get to Hollywood?'"

Adam didn't finish Grade 12, but he found work playing extras in movies and TV.

At 19, he landed the lead role in *Squanto*. Halfway through shooting in Montreal, Adam become extremely lonely.

"He phoned me and said he was going to quit," recalled Chris. "I said, 'You can't do that now. If you come home, you can kiss acting goodbye.'"

Instead, three carloads of cousins drove to Montreal to stay with him. They lived together for five weeks until Adam finished the movie.

At Lake Manitoba First Nation, his accomplishments seem unreal to people — that someone from their midst could go on to such celebrity and acclaim.

Adam's uncle Allan Swan mentions the time he got a call from Adam. "He was on a street in New York with a cell phone," he said, as if that was almost beyond comprehension.

Added his Aunt Marlene: "It's hard to believe that's little Adam, when you're watching him" on TV or on the big theatre screen.

"[Adam] was hyper as a child but in a cute way," said Marlene. That was so like Sally. "She was hyper, too. She had all the energy," said Allan.

Adam Beach

Both Sally and Adam were second-born children in their families, if you believe there's anything to birth order.

A new movie by Adam is a big event on Lake Manitoba First Nation. About 30 relatives from both Allan's and Marlene's side of the family went to see *Flags of Our Fathers* together in Winnipeg. Uncle Allan makes sure he's parked in front of the television set whenever Adam is on.

The non-aboriginal community here is also proud of Adam, and amazed at what he's managed to overcome. "It would set some people off completely if they had that thrust on them. He's risen above it," said Paul Johnson, a farmer in the area and husband to Adam's former teacher, Bev.

His bond with his brothers, Chris and David, is deeper and stronger than most. "My brothers have always been like mother and father to me," Adam said from Los Angeles. He agreed to a telephone interview.

Growing up without parents, "there was a side of me that said nobody was going to take anything from me again," Adam said. "You feel like you're a lone warrior, and no one understands the emotions you're feeling."

Today, Adam takes being a role model for aboriginal youth seriously. "I'm pretty grounded," he said.

He speaks to aboriginal youths across North America. His speeches used to be about setting goals and following your dreams. Now, he talks about being responsible for your actions.

"I tell them, 'You're the decision-maker. It's up to you. If you want to drink, I can't stop you. Just don't blame it on anybody else.'

"I'll say, 'I don't want you to do it, but I can't tell you what to do.' And then I'll tell how my mother died.

"And I'll say, 'Hopefully, if their choice is drinking, it's in a safe environment.'"

* * *

Because Sally had won at bingo that night, she stopped at the store on her way home and bought bags of chips, soft drinks and other treats for her kids. One can imagine her crossing the road and already anticipating the looks on her boys' faces when she walked in the door with her goodies.

The chips and drinks and treats were scattered across the road in front of her house when help arrived.

Another irony is Sally and Dennis were preparing to move to Winnipeg. There would be more opportunities for work for Dennis in the city.

The family's bags were already packed. Dennis's brother, Chris, had already bought the house. Dennis went to look at it. It was a fixer-upper and he planned to do that. The possession date was June 15, but the house was empty and the seller said they could move in.

Adam says he doesn't remember any of the events of that tragic period, and that he probably blocked them out.

A reporter once asked him why he smiles so easily, and Adam said that it was from the habit of masking the pain of his childhood. But it seems he may have inherited it. His mom smiled all the time, and all the Beach boys smile like that, like their mom.

Chris's mother-in-law, Dorothy Baptiste, went to school with Sally. "She was always laughing. She was always singing," she said. "She was never sad. She was always in a happy mood. And she was so pretty."

Dennis and Sally Beach initially raised their three boys in what was a third world shack with one bedroom and no running water. The potty was on the porch.

Yet, she was the one lifting other peoples' spirits, taking an interest in others. People wondered how in the world she did it.

Angel, the wife of Adam's brother, Chris, has found it interesting getting to know the three Beach brothers. "They're the same, always happy and really nice. They're really nice people," she said.

Chris sings and plays guitar, as does his youngest brother David, who plays in a band called X-Status.

Chris is a great example of the Beach brothers. He has been plagued with health problems since before his mother died. He contracted rheumatic fever which went into his brain and effected his memory and learning abilities. He suffered an array of symptoms and for a time couldn't even remember his name. Today, he suffers seizures.

But he is still a Beach. You can tell by his ready smile and positive outlook.

* * *

One of the mysteries of Sally's death is why she lay on the side of the road for more than two hours before an ambulance arrived. It was wet and drizzling out. People knew enough not to move the body. They covered her with a blanket.

Even if she couldn't be saved, an ambulance might have kept her alive long enough to save her baby.

Family members say when someone phoned the Ashern ambulance service, the caller was asked if Sally had treaty status. The federal government pays ambulance costs for aboriginals with treaty status. But Sally did not have treaty status. Back then, an aboriginal woman lost her status if she married a non-treaty husband.

According to family, the ambulance service was mad at Vogar. Emergency services had provided an ambulance to Vogar recently and not been paid.

The RCMP arrived but there was still no ambulance. The RCMP then phoned Ashern. It isn't known what transpired but apparently Ashern ambulance wasn't coming. An ambulance from Lundar, 25 kilometres far-ther away than Ashern, was summoned. The Lundar emergency crew didn't know the area and got lost. They went to an address across the street in Lake Manitoba First Nation, instead of across from the school in Vogar.

Donna Steinthorson, who retired from nursing last year, said it's possible the Ashern ambulance didn't show up because of fears the family couldn't pay.

When Steinthorson arrived at about 11:30 p.m., Sally still had a faint pulse. A woman so far along in her pregnancy cannot withstand that kind of trauma, Steinthorson said. "She's more vulnerable to internal injuries. She would have had severe internal injuries. When you're flung like that, she would have been unconscious from head injuries, too."

While some of the story might be starting to sound like shades of the tragic death of Helen Betty Osborne, it should be pointed out that the driver of the vehicle that struck Sally was aboriginal.

The driver who struck Sally hid in the woods that night and turned himself in the next morning. People believe he was driving while intoxicated, and even the Wikipedia site for Adam Beach claims he was, but he was not convicted of drunk driving. He was sentenced to six months in jail for dangerous driving, driving without a licence and leaving the scene of an accident. The court, by petition of both sides of the family, awarded $38,000 from insurance coverage.

For the driver's father, who was in a common-law marriage with the mother, the incident seemed to be the last straw. He sat on the sofa with Dennis Beach after Sally's funeral trying to convey how sorry he was. He left his family shortly after.

Alice Roulette of Winnipeg only wishes her sister, Sally, was still alive today to see how well her three boys turned out. Eldest of the three Beach boys, Chris, 37, and wife, Angel, recently had twin daughters and named them Sally and Anne, after his mother, Sally Anne Beach.

But Alice is glad Sally's parents, Adam's grandparents Barney and Florence Swan, lived to see Adam's success. In 1994, a huge family contingent drove to Winnipeg to see the premiere of *Squanto*, Adam's first movie. Adam's grandmother, Florence, sat in the darkened theatre and cried.

Lower Fort Garry is the oldest stone fur-trading post in North America

History

LEGEND OF THE GREAT GOLD ROBBERY
March 29, 2004

TREHERNE — Betty Gates defended her brother Ken Leishman to the hilt against accusations that he was involved in the Winnipeg International Airport great gold robbery.

Little did she know her brother was preparing to stash $4 million in bullion virtually under her nose.

Gates, nee Leishman, recalled the sensational gold robbery orchestrated by her brother almost 40 years ago. Gates still lives in Treherne, 110 kilometres west of Winnipeg, where the Leishman family grew up.

"I thought people were nasty to suggest Ken might be behind the gold robbery," recalled Gates, 75. "Oh God, I was so sure Ken was honest and would not do things like that again."

On March 1, 1966, Leishman masterminded one of the biggest gold heists in modern history: 12 gold ingots weighing up to 92 pounds each, worth an estimated $4 million (in 1966 dollars) on the black market in Hong Kong, where Leishman intended to sell the gold.

Three days after the robbery, Leishman wanted to move the gold from an accomplice's freezer and stash it near his home town of Treherne. But a weather system changed his mind — the blizzard of March 4, 1966, one of the worst blizzards in Manitioba history. Leishman couldn't make it to Treherne so he dropped the gold in the Riverview backyard of the accomplice. The blizzard buried the gold under an eight-foot snowbank.

"I was aghast," said Gates, when her brother was arrested a few days

Betty Gates holds news clipping of her famous brother, Ken Leishman

later for the gold robbery, and eventually convicted. "He was going straight. I was so sure he'd learned his lesson."

Leishman was a logical suspect because of his previous conviction as the Gentleman Bandit. Leishman would board a commercial airliner to Toronto in the morning, rob a bank in the afternoon, mail the loot back to his North Kildonan house, and hop a flight back to Winnipeg that evening.

What almost made Gates more angry was the fact that Ken went bowling the night before the gold heist with his brother Bob, a Winnipeg policeman. Police even searched Bob's house for the gold, adding to his humiliation.

"I held that against him. Ken knew what was going on and he took out his brother like that," she said.

Yet the happy-go-lucky Leishman was liked by nearly everyone, even the police who dealt with him. The day after the gold robbery, he was stopped at a red light next to a police cruiser. Leishman rolled down his window and exchanged greetings with the officers.

"Ken was personable," said Gates. "When he was picking up bales, he could get 10 other kids to help him."

Their parents were poor and split up when Ken was barely two years old. Gates remembers being so poor the kids would dip rhubarb sticks into salt instead of sugar because they couldn't afford sugar. Ken spent some time in foster homes.

"It's not like kids today where your parents are behind you. We were always in the way."

The family moved to downtown Winnipeg and Ken started to hang around with a bad gang of kids. They stole oranges from Eaton's, and Ken would also pilfer the odd comic book. So the family moved back to Treherne, partly to keep him out of trouble.

Leishman's capture in the gold robbery wasn't the end of his story. He escaped from Headingley Correctional Institution, stole a plane, and was eventually recaptured in Gary, Indiana.

During his escape, Betty's 16-year-old son pulled into the driveway one night in Treherne and was hauled out of the car at gunpoint by Mounties, who thought he was his uncle.

"We loved Ken, and we just felt so sorry," his sister said.

Leishman served his prison time and started a new life for himself and wife Elva in Red Lake, Ontario, north of Kenora. He became president of the local chamber of commerce, and lost a bid to become mayor.

He died on December 14, 1979, when the Medevac plane he was piloting crashed in poor weather near Thunder Bay. He was flying an aboriginal woman from northern Ontario to a hospital.

Betty said the legacy of her brother Ken has been to make members of the Leishmans and her own family "so sickeningly honest. We're always thinking that someone will suspect we're up to something."

"My kids will say, 'Mom, why did you teach us not to lie? Everyone else can tell a lie and we can't.'"

"I never believed in telling a lie but now I think, with these telemarketers, you have to sometimes."

None of the Leishman and Gates children have shown an inclination toward crime, and "are all honest, hard-working people," Gates said. Three of Ken Leishman's children are regular members of the Mormon Church.

One comment Ken made as a child seemed to sum up his attitude. "Ken was sitting on Grandpa's knee, and he said, 'You know, Grandpa, some day I'd like to have lots of money like you have. But I don't want to have to work as hard as you.'

"Ken was only six or seven years old at the time."

BLOOD ON THE PRAIRIE
November 4, 2001

TURTLE MOUNTAIN — The 77 Métis men, including boys as young as 12, watched with fingers on their rifle triggers as the Sioux army gathered along the crest of the hill.

"A mass of plumed warriors which appeared like a totality of the Sioux nation were silhouetted against the horizon," wrote Manitoba's most famous historian, W.L. Morton.

An estimated 2,000 to 2,500 Sioux amassed on a land formation called Grand Coteau, in northeastern North Dakota, part of the Missouri Plateau that extends north to Manitoba's Turtle Mountain. Morton described the Sioux army as having "war ponies of piebald and pinto and chestnut vivid on the skyline, their gun barrels and spear points glinting in the fierce sunlight."

Then they charged.

The clash would be the bloodiest plains battle in Manitoba or North Dakota history, and ranked with some of the bloodiest to take place in North America.

Yet what looked like a sure massacre of the Métis — every man, woman and child took absolution the night before — was to turn into the most stunning military victory in Manitoba Métis history.

Morton: "Here and there a Sioux warrior whirled from his saddle and tumbled into the grass."

Abbe George Dugas, a missionary priest in Manitoba who heard accounts of the battle from survivors, wrote that Sioux warriors lay "strew-

Steve Racine in the Turtle Mountain area

ing the yellow prairie with their heaving bodies."

Among the marksmen was 13-year-old Gabriel Dumont, who would go on to become chief of Métis hunters in Saskatchewan, and who famously lead the Métis military in the Northwest Rebellion of 1885.

Morton estimated 80 Sioux warriors died in the Battle of Grand Coteau. Some Métis claim the death toll may have been up to 200, which would place the battle on a scale with Little Big Horn.

Yet the battle is not widely known. That may be because neither the Métis buffalo hunters nor the Sioux were diarists and chroniclers like the British, but rather relied on oral storytelling. As well, the battle wasn't near a population centre.

The year 2001 marked its 150th anniversary.

The dwindling bison herds brought the combatants together that summer of 1851. The bison herds in the Red River Valley were nearly hunted to extinction. Métis hunters were pushing farther west to hunt, threatening the Assiniboine Sioux, who depended on the Turtle Mountain bison for their food.

Métis brigades usually hunted individually but three brigades of Métis buffalo hunters ventured out together that summer: the Red River brigade, the Pembina brigade, and the brigade from St. Francois Xavier, the smallest of the three. St. Francois Xavier, today a bedroom community just west of Winnipeg, began as a Métis community run by Cuthbert Grant.

The brigades travelled in three columns spread 30 to 50 kilometres apart, "like tines on a fork," said James Ritchie, a local historian based in Boissevain. That was so they wouldn't miss any bison but also so a brigade could send for help within a day's ride should Sioux attack.

The Métis knew they were going into Sioux territory, and the Sioux were the most feared warriors on the plains. The Assiniboine Sioux claimed territory that extended from Minot to Brandon, up to the Assiniboine River that's named after them. This is the approximate range of the Turtle Mountain buffalo herd on which the tribe depended, said Ritchie.

The Métis and Sioux had already skirmished in 1849. Hunting parties from each side collided while hunting the same buffalo herd near where Boissevain is today, in what's called the Battle of Buck's Hill. The two sides were more interested in hunting than war, however, and negotiated a temporary truce.

In the summer of 1851, the brigades met up somewhere between Pembina, North Dakota. and Star Mound near the southern Manitoba town of Snowflake, then travelled southwest in their columns.

The St. Francis Xavier brigade was the northernmost of the three brigades and would have been hugging the southern edge of Turtle Mountain inside North Dakota. That's where the Battle of Grand Coteau began, on Dog Den Butte, about 100 kilometres south of the Canada–U.S. border, straight south of Deloraine.

"The battle of 1851 is a watershed. The Métis don't know how strong they are until they are tested, whereas the Sioux people still think they are a power," said Ritchie.

It was an extraordinarily one-sided battle — but not for the side you would think.

The body of Jean Baptiste Malaterre, a Métis scout, was found shot with 67 arrows and three bullets in the first day of fighting. Malaterre's limbs were cut off, as were some organs, which several Sioux speared on to their lances and waved at Métis during the six-hour battle.

Yet remarkably, Malaterre was the only known Métis fatality.

The Métis used their Red River carts like a portable fort. They placed them in a circle, axle to axle, and tilted up slightly, with the fronts facing out so the shafts pointed out like spears. Trenches were dug beneath the carts where women and children huddled for safety. Similar crude trenches acting as rifle pits were dug just in front of the carts, with the soil piles in front. It made for little ramparts behind which the Métis hunters lay like snipers and shot their mounted attackers.

The livestock remained inside the circled wagons. The women reloaded rifles and passed them from underneath the carts to the sharpshooters.

The Sioux mode of attack, as would be seen in the battle with U.S. Cavalry General George Custer, was to swarm and simply overwhelm opponents. But that's not how the Assiniboine Sioux fought against the Métis. The Sioux military strategy was largely a bow-and-arrow attack, with some rifles mixed in. They were experts at using the bow-and-arrow on horseback, guiding the horse with their knees, but that mode of attack was folly at Grand Coteau.

"The Sioux used hit-and-run, guerilla warfare," said Steve Racine, president of the Turtle Mountain local chapter of the Manitoba Métis Federation. Racine knows both the written and oral history of the battle. "They hit their target and moved back. That was effective [against] bows and arrows, but it wasn't a good plan for fighting [against] rifles. Some of the buffalo guns could shoot 300 metres."

Morton questioned why the Sioux didn't attack en masse that first day as was their custom. Instead, they repeatedly attacked in small groups. The Métis buffalo hunters — legendary sharpshooters — picked off Sioux riders one after another. The Métis had the technological advantage of more numerous and superior rifles. The Sioux had difficulty getting close enough to get in range for their older rifles and were already having to ration ammunition by the second day.

The Métis brigade heard whoops and war songs from the Sioux camp the night before the first day's battle. By the next night, songs of mourning were mixed with cries for revenge.

The battle ran over two days for certain, July 13–14, 1851, and possibly longer. The Métis hunters were able to erect their mobile forts with amazing speed. On the battle's second day, they tried to flee and folded into their mini fort on the fly as the Sioux descended on them. It was the same devastating result for the Sioux.

Métis enforcements from the other brigades are believed to have arrived at the end of the second day of fighting, by which time the Sioux had conceded defeat.

Historians believe the number of casualties on the Sioux side was simply too ridiculous for the Sioux to continue. There was still only one known Métis killed, although many were wounded, including Gabriel Dumont's father. Both sides had lost numerous livestock, mainly horses, but again the Sioux lost many more than the Métis.

Sioux accounts are hard to come by. The Assiniboine Sioux have scattered into Saskatchewan and Alberta.

Dakota Tipi Chief Dennis Pashe contends the battle was only a minor skirmish grossly exaggerated by the Métis. He maintained there were only a few deaths on either side, in a recent letter to aboriginal newspaper *Grassroots*. Pashe was responding to a Métis account of the battle printed in the paper. Pashe could not be reached for further comment.

Most historians and Métis people don't agree with Pashe's version. Racine tends towards the high end, believing up to 200 Sioux may have died. "I don't think the Sioux would have given up the territory for anything less than that," Racine said.

The Sioux gave up a territory they had controlled for up to 250 years. The same Sioux had escorted explorer La Vérendrye across the territory a century earlier.

Now the Métis controlled the area and the coveted Turtle Mountain bison herd.

But that would end, too. "Roughly 30 years later [in 1883], the last bison of the Turtle Mountain herd was reported killed at Whitewater Lake," said Ritchie.

* * *

"We are descendants of the Battle of Grand Coteau," said Racine, waving an arm over the Turtle Mountain area where a Métis community of about 300 live today. "If the Métis had lost, we wouldn't be here today."

Racine, a local history enthusiast, has appeared in three episodes of CBC's, *A Peoples' History*, playing an aboriginal man, an aboriginal woman, and a Métis man. He has also been consulted on Métis history by the show's producers.

Racine's great-great-grandfather in St. Francois Xavier would have been a child on that buffalo hunt. Whole communities went on the buffalo hunts, except the infirm. While the St. Francois hunters numbered only 77, there were 315 people altogether counting women and children.

Norman Fleury, 52, also Métis, was told of the Battle of Grand Coteau by his grandmother when he was a child. He never saw or heard a word about it again until 10 years ago when he read Morton's account. He felt a wave of emotion come over him.

He, too, wants Métis people to know the story and take pride in their ancestors, but not at the expense of aboriginal people.

"We don't want to tell it to insult the Sioux people. The Sioux were great warriors," said Fleury, who lives in a little hamlet west of Brandon called Woodnorth.

The other effect of the Battle of Grand Coteau was to create political conditions that led to a rapprochement between the different parties in Manitoba, said Ritchie. In 1860, the Hudson Bay Company and British Army brokered a five-part treaty between themselves and the Métis, Dakota Sioux and Saulteaux/Ojibway.

"This treaty is very significant because the Battle of Grand Coteau is the last time these parties fought each other in battle," said Ritchie. "So it was a lasting peace which paved the way for peaceful settlement of the prairies."

The Battle of Grand Coteau also explains why Louis Riel, in 1870, was able to stand up to Canada in the Red River Rebellion.

That was Morton's conclusion after researching Grand Coteau. Morton maintained the Métis buffalo hunters exemplified the discipline and military organization that would later allow Riel to turn back Central Canada's bid to control Manitoba.

"The Battle of Grand Coteau was perhaps the proudest memory of the Métis nation…Nothing more conclusively proved their mastery of the plains," wrote Morton.

"Their conduct on the march of the cart brigade, their plains craft, their battle tactics, from the firing from the saddle to the use of the rifle pit, were brilliant by any standard of warfare."

History is more debatable than we newspaper writers give it credit for. For that reason, some changes have been made to the original story.

TUNNEL NETWORK: FOR BOOTLEGGING OR BEATING DRAFT?
July 30, 2006

ELMA — During the Second World War, young men avoiding conscription arrived in this railway town hoping to "disappear."

They roomed upstairs at Peter and Anna Kolega's house behind their pool hall on Highway 15, 75 kilomeres east of Winnipeg. If authorities came knocking, they could escape into a network of at least 50 metres of underground tunnels that start in the basement coal bin. The concrete tunnels, some of which can still be viewed today, had at least three escape hatches.

The men stayed with the Kolegas until the couple found a railway conductor, perhaps through bribery, to transport their guests to bush camps in Northern Ontario where no one asked questions.

That's one of the more intriguing tales told about the mysterious tunnels Peter Kolega built under his property 70 years ago.

"I'm just telling you what their grandson told me," said Pearl Stelko, who lived next door to the Kolegas for many years. The grandson, Bobby Kolega, was the son of a daughter born out of wedlock and raised by the Kolegas. He is dead now, but at one point he went to jail for writing bad cheques.

The Kolega's pool hall still fronts Highway 15 in Elma. Frank Smerch has owned the property for the past decade and tries to preserve it, although he is in his 80s now. You can poke your head into the basement coal bin and still see the tunnel run at least 10 metres east before it turns. You can look the other way and see it run for about five metres west before it turns, too. A person could still crawl through the tunnels — with difficulty — but that doesn't seem wise after so many years and much ground shifting.

There's no doubt the Kolegas were engaged in smuggling, particularly homebrew. People could either go there and casually buy a small pop bottle filled with spirits, or larger quantities. "Mom would get all excited because Dad would disappear, going to have 'refreshments.' Oh, the women would get angry," Stelko said.

In the case of police surveillance or a raid, a customer could crawl from the house to the dance hall, or vice versa. Or the customer could crawl to a little oil shed next to the pool hall where the Kolegas sold oil and gasoline, climb out, and run. There are stories of a fourth passageway in the pool hall but Smerch has never found it.

"You could be out of the house, into the oil shed, and out onto the street, and there was nothing police could do," said one long-time area resident.

Frank Smerch looks down a bootlegging tunnel in Elma

Kolega built a foot-high concrete fence along much of the tunnel, with open pockets, apparently to allow in air. There is still a six-inch diameter air pipe in the yard poking out of the ground, like a historic marker.

Even without the tunnels, the house Kolega constructed is amazing. It's made almost entirely of hand-mixed concrete. The inside walls are overlaid with concrete, instead of plaster. Even the ceilings are concrete. Kolega paid kids a few pennies to collect tin cans, then opened them and nailed them onto the wood framing. He then laid concrete over the tin. No one can explain this peculiar choice of building materials.

The pool hall is also a concrete fortress. An inside stairway is made of solid concrete as if built for outside. The pool hall's concrete foundation is a metre wide. "This place will stand for another 100 years," Smerch said. Even the outhouse is concrete.

It was a poor community, but the Kolegas always seemed to have more money than other business owners, Stelko said.

"Nobody got to know them too well. [Peter Kolega] was such an unassuming man. Very quiet. Nobody would think it," she said.

And very discreet. "You can't get away from it. He was a nice man. But there was a reason for it. He didn't want to ruffle feathers."

Peter died in 1960, and Anna in 1966, both in the house. The family held onto ownership of the house until the early 1980s. It has changed hands a couple of times since.

Reached in Richmond, B.C., Patricia Cartwright, 82, one of three surviving children of Peter and Anna Kolega, scoffed at the stories surrounding her mom and dad. "My parents wouldn't do anything like that," she said.

"My dad was a wonderful guy. My mother was wonderful, too. They were just the most wonderful people."

Then how does she explain the tunnels? "What tunnels? What are you talking about?" she responded. Cartwright left home to attend high school in Winnipeg in the late 1930s. "Not in my parents' place. There were never any tunnels. I've never heard of such nonsense."

BOOZE, BRIBES AND BROADS
June 29, 2008

RIDING MOUNTAIN NATIONAL PARK — They made alcohol and hid the still in the medical building.

They bought off the camp superintendent and guards with bottles of liquor. They attended Saturday night dances in nearby towns, Ohla for one, and had relations with some of the local women.

The German prisoners of war even got their hands on firearms to go hunting.

Booze, bribes and broads, in the vernacular of those Second World War times. This was a Prisoner of War camp? The Whitewater German PoW camp in Riding Mountain National Park sounds more like a German version of the TV series *Hogan's Heroes*.

The escapades of Manitoba's largest PoW camp in the Second World War are detailed in Ed Stozek's self-published book, *The Sawmill Boys, PoWs and Conscientious Objectors: Stories from the Parkland*.

The sawmill camp was composed of 450 German soldiers captured in North Africa. Local old-timers told Stozek how the German prisoners arrived in the fall of 1943: in the back of trucks, lustily belting out German songs.

Among them was Josef Gabski, 87, and living in California when this was written. Gabski never forgot the generosity of Canadians and the liberties afforded the PoWs.

"I think we had more food to eat than the Canadians," said Gabski, who made a nostalgic return to the former camp in 1993.

Canoe carved by PoWs

The prisoners were assigned to hard labour, cutting cordwood to heat Manitoba homes. It was before power tools. PoWs used axes and crosscut saws. The wood alleviated fuel

Whitewater PoW camp in Riding Mountain. Joe Gabski on far left.

shortages in places such as Brandon, Dauphin and Winnipeg.

The PoWs were paid, albeit a meagre 30 cents a day. At one point, prisoners went on strike. The men had saved enough to order pyjamas through the Eaton's catalogue and suspected Canadian authorities were withholding their purchases. The pyjamas eventually arrived.

Sports equipment and musical instruments were provided by the International Red Cross. PoWs formed a 12-piece band and organized soccer teams.

PoWs learned from a magazine how to make a canoe and made a dozen by hollowing out giant spruce trees. Some rotted-out canoes can still be found on the shore of Whitewater Lake, where the camp was based, near the centre of Riding Mountain park.

PoWs used to cross the lake in their canoes and once returned with a passenger: a bear cub that became the camp mascot.

"We built a cage for it, and one guy was assigned as the bear keeper," Gabski said in a telephone interview from California.

The bear provided many hours of entertainment. It disappeared the second winter, only to be found in the spring hibernating beneath a camp building. It got up, shambled over to the kitchen and made a horrible mess. The camp superintendent was reprimanded by superiors.

There was plenty of recreation time. The Germans loved to trek the trails throughout Riding Mountain woods. There were no fences. In winter, they snowshoed and

Joe Gabski official camp mug shot.

ME 050033
CAMP 133
30-3-43

cross-country skied. They occasionally hunted rabbits for dinner.

Prisoners would visit farms and small towns at the edge of the park. The PoWs also endeared themselves to farmers with cheap labour at harvest time.

Relationships were formed. Farmers were known to take their PoW threshers to the local pub. Some prisoners attended church. They would sit in the back pews at the Ukrainian Catholic Church in Oakburn.

Gabski recalled the moonshine, or white alcohol. A PoW dentist at the medical station was in charge of alcohol production. "Sometimes it tasted pretty rough, but what the hell — it was alcohol," Gabski said. Stozek has heard stories that prisoners even made a crude schnapps using cherry pie filling.

Sugar was rationed during wartime. That made it hard for some Ukrainian farmers to make their famous potato whisky. But PoWs had a surplus of sugar, perhaps from Red Cross care packages. Bartering began. For sugar, farmers paid with items such as homemade bread, potatoes, pork and tobacco.

The PoWs were allowed to send one postcard home each year. Most let family know they were alive but many also related how well Canadians were treating them.

Why such generous treatment for the PoWs? The feeling among many in Canada was that the German prisoners were largely conscripts to Hitler's army.

Riding Mountain National Park was also surrounded by mostly Ukrainian farmers who "felt a connection" to the Germans because of their proximity to Ukraine in Europe, Stozek said. Stozek guided me on

Ed Stozek at Whitewater PoW camp in Riding Mountain

a 10-kilometre off-road mountain bike ride to the former camp.

It was different with some English farmers. One story is of an English farmer who repeatedly cussed and berated the PoWs hired to thresh his wheat crop. The PoWs got back at him, placing all his wheat stooks upside down.

Many Ukrainians were also less than fond of the English authorities running Canada. Ukrainian men couldn't find work or lost their jobs to returning English servicemen. And nearly 1,000 Ukrainian-Canadians were interned in a hockey arena in Brandon in the First World War. The internment was because the Ukrainians traced their roots back to a part of Ukraine that was under Austrian rule.

"I'm sure there were still bitter feelings from that by the time the Second World War rolled around," Stozek said.

Some PoWs snuck out of the camp on weekends to attend dances in nearby towns. The guard dogs were easy to get past. PoWs befriended them with treats.

At the dances, romantic liaisons formed. It is uncertain how far those liaisons went — perhaps it just gave them something to dream about. PoWs would hitch rides with locals back to their camp so they could make it in time for morning roll call.

The PoWs came from all walks of life. Many had trades, like Gabski, who was a machinist. Gabski was one of 48 men in his class. All went to war. Only nine returned.

There were also teachers, academics, a watchmaker, artists, musicians and electronics experts. One of the navy men built a homemade radio, allegedly to communicate with Germany. Guards eventually followed a trail through the snow and found the radio hidden in a woodpile, Gabski said.

"When you're locked up like that with a whole bunch of guys with different skills, it's amazing what you can do," he said.

There were some hard-core Nazis among the inmates — "idiots," Gabski called them — who tried to organize men to take over the camp, without success.

"What was the point?" said Gabski. Most of the hard-core Nazis were found out and shipped to PoW camps in Alberta where security was tougher. There were only a couple of escapes from the Whitewater camp. The farthest anyone got before recapture was Winnipeg.

The PoW camp was composed of 15 buildings, including six bunkhouses capable of sleeping 100 men each. The barracks were heated by wood stoves.

After the camp closed in November 1945, local people salvaged what they could. What remained was burned to the ground. There are still some ruins — crumbling foundations, broken bricks and rusty tin cans and stove pipes. Beds of purple irises and baby's breath that the PoWs planted still blossom each summer.

Stozek deserves credit for self-publishing a book and preserving this part of Manitoba history. The book also covers early forestry in Riding Mountain and the conscientious-objector camp.

Gabski is a VIP invitee to Riding Mountain National Park's 75th anniversary celebration on July 26. However, poor health will keep him from attending.

SOME FACTS ON POW CAMPS IN CANADA:

- More than 37,000 PoWs were placed in 40 remote camps across Canada during the Second World War.
- The largest PoW camps were in Alberta, at Medicine Hat, with 12,000 prisoners, and Lethbridge, with 15,000.
- A smaller PoW forestry camp was at Mafeking, north of Swan River, with about 150 prisoners, and another at Pine Falls.

LOST IN THE WILDERNESS
July 23, 2006

BOISSEVAIN — Just over 200 years ago this summer, John Pritchard got lost.

It was mid-June, 1805. Pritchard, who had arrived from England in 1800 and had little experience living off the land, wandered away from his campsite. He had no food, blanket, knife, rifle or horse. Just a flint stone and the clothes on his back.

So began his biblical-like 40-day odyssey in the prairie wilderness — and one of Manitoba's most incredible survival stories.

A naked Pritchard, long given up for dead, would finally stagger out of the tall prairie grass into the camp of an aboriginal family. He had been naked for all but the first days of his ordeal. His skin was sun-blistered and mercilessly ravaged with mosquito and other insect bites, and his eyes were haunted. He was so starved you could see the bones through his flesh.

The Assiniboine Sioux family who found him initially thought he was a ghost. They called him *cheepi*, meaning "the corpse." Then they saved his life.

Despite the current fascination with survival stories, Pritchard's story is little known in Manitoba (even though a stately old school on Henderson Highway in Winnipeg is named after him on land he later farmed).

Several Winnipeg-based historians contacted by the *Free Press* were unaware of Pritchard's tortured history.

That's not surprising since Manitoba history tends to be Winnipeg-centric, said James Ritchie, a local historian in southwestern Manitoba, who helped the *Free Press* retrace Pritchard's footsteps.

With the luxury of a motor vehicle, Ritchie and I followed Pritchard's agonized wanderings, starting from the confluence of the Assiniboine and Souris rivers, about 175 kilometres west of Winnipeg. From there, we travelled west nearly to the Saskatchewan border (we didn't go into Saskatchewan the way Pritchard did), then back going diagonally southeast to Boissevain.

* * *

Who was John Pritchard? The summer he got lost, he was just 28 and a well-liked clerk at fur-trading XY Company (which later joined North West Company) at Fort La Souris, just east of Brandon.

On June 11, Pritchard and a companion had started out for a North West Company trading post, just west of the confluence of the Qu'Appelle and Assiniboine rivers, near where the town of Esterhazy, Saskatchewan, is today. The companion wanted to deliver two horses to the fort, and, if lucky, find a horse stolen from him. The companion believed the horse was nabbed by Assiniboine Sioux. The Assiniboine Sioux were reputed as the greatest horse thieves among Plains Indians — or the worst, depending on your perspective — wrote Lawrence B. Clarke in *Souris Valley Plains: A*

John Pritchard kills a grouse with a stick

History, in a local self-published account of Pritchard's story.

Pritchard and his companion were unable to hire a Métis guide, as planned, and after four days of travel and not reaching the Qu'Appelle River, wished they had. They realized they'd gone astray. Instead of travelling diagonally northwest, they'd gone due west. They decided they had better return home.

That night, the companion forgot to tie up the horses and they ran off. The companion gave chase, leaving Pritchard, who was lame from an accident the previous winter, alone at the campsite. Neither the horses nor friend returned, and the next morning Pritchard walked to a hill a good distance off to make a fire to help his companion find his way back.

Pritchard found himself surrounded by dense woods. A heavy thunderstorm ensued and he couldn't use the sun to find his way back to camp. He couldn't even find his former campsite. That evening he found a creek and followed it, assuming it drained into the Assiniboine River. Once he found the Assiniboine, he reckoned, he would follow it northwest to Qu'Appelle and reach the trading post.

But he assumed wrong. The creek didn't empty into the Assiniboine. It was Pipestone Creek that empties into the Souris River, and which runs southeast, not northwest. Pritchard followed the creek and travelled in completely the opposite direction from the Esterhazy-area trading post.

"That's what happens when you don't hire a Métis guide," joked Steve Racine, president of the Turtle Mountain chapter of the Manitoba Métis Federation.

While on our trek, Ritchie and I happened to bump into Racine at the Co-op gas station in Boissevain. Racine said there is some truth to the stereotype that white settlers were inept in wilderness skills compared to aboriginal people.

Yet Racine understood how a person could become so confused.

Pritchard would eventually see the Turtle Mountains on the horizon, and still think he was headed into Qu'Appelle Valley. "I was lost once as a youngster. Panic sets in, and, in a state of anxiety, it's amazing what you will think," said Racine.

Pritchard's condition deteriorated from the first day. He didn't even have proper boots; they fell apart after a few days. Pritchard was also short, and grasses and thistle were much higher in those days, up to the chests of horses, as artist George Catlin proclaimed on a trek through the prairies in the 1830s. It would have been difficult for Pritchard to look down and watch where he stepped.

So he wrapped his feet in his shirt and pants to protect them from thistles and other plants. By the tenth day, he was stark naked except for his hat. Spear grass barbs still bloodied his feet with cuts, and his legs would swell up from infernal Canada thistle needles.

"My legs had the appearance of a porcupine," he wrote in an account of his ordeal, published most recently in *Beaver* magazine in June 1942.

"Pritchard was such a greenhorn!" exclaimed Ritchie.

Retracing his steps, you can't help but try to imagine the desolation and despair Pritchard must have felt.

The southwestern corner of Manitoba was not yet inhabited by any settlers in 1805. Americans Lewis and Clark were in the midst of their Voyage of Discovery just to the south. The vista we saw extended 5 to 10 kilometres in all directions. Pritchard limped along hour after hour, day after day, under a hot sun, or in rain, without seeing a single living soul.

Bison were everywhere — Pritchard was frustrated at seeing them at

James Ritchie on the hill
Pritchard saw on his 32nd day

every marsh and small lake and not having the means to kill one for food.

None of the small islands of forest on the landscape today existed in Pritchard's time. Prairie fires would have taken care of that, Ritchie explained.

Wolves and eagles followed him, Pritchard wrote, waiting for him to die. He notched a stick with his teeth to mark "each miserable night."

He slept badly, usually on wet ground — it rained every second day, preventing him from using his flint stone to make smudge fires to ward off mosquitoes. He sometimes slept under deadfall. Flies and every type of creepy crawly would have plagued him.

Including wood ticks. On a short 10-metre jaunt through tall quack grass by the Souris River that Pritchard traversed, my pant legs were blanketed with wood ticks. I ran back to the gravel road and did the "wood ticks jig," flicking off at least 40 of them. I found six more once inside the car, and three more back in my hotel room, which I killed by splicing them with my plastic calling card while talking with my wife on the phone. These options weren't available to Pritchard.

Pritchard passed south of Oak Lake, likely traversing near towns that exist today, like Grande-Clairiere. He forded the Souris River, for some reason, and kept going through the Lauder Sand Hills. He lived on frogs, and occasionally robbed bird nests for eggs and young birds.

His secret to survival? He didn't really have one. He believed in God. That's where he gave credit.

Talkative, cheerful and optimistic, Pritchard believed God had blessed him with good spirits. Several times during his ordeal he would lay down on the grass and hope to die. But a change of attitude would come over him, and he would get up again and struggle on. (It's reminiscent of Chief Dan George's character in the movie *Little Big Man*, who repeatedly lies down and declares, "It's a good day to die," only to get up a while later and decide it was a better day to live.)

After being lost for about 25 days, when Pritchard was so weak he could barely stand up, a grouse flew straight at him. Pritchard feebly tossed a stick at it, miraculously hitting the bird and killing it. It provided him with two days of sustenance. He believed it was a sign from God.

"It was not I that killed it, it was the Almighty, for I had not then sufficient strength. I threw myself upon the ground and poured out thanks to the Giver of all goodness."

On about the 30th day, he thought he spotted a group of aboriginal people in the distance, far away from where he planned to travel, and made a beeline for them. When he arrived at the spot, there was nothing there. It was a mirage, he determined. But as he gathered firewood to camp, he stumbled upon two old wintering homes for a trading post, the first sign of human life he'd seen. He exulted. He'd arrived at Qu'Appelle! God had guided him.

Yet something was wrong. He noticed tar on some rope, a practise of Hudson Bay posts to make rope more durable. Qu'Appelle was a Nor'Wester post. There was also a peculiar design of sleigh. "Good God!" he exclaimed. It was a Hudson Bay post. He was at Whitewater Lake, west of where Boissevain is today.

He at least knew where he was but was starving to death. On the 33rd day, he spotted two aboriginal boys. He waved an old boot he'd taken from the trading post on a stick to get their attention. When the boys approached, Pritchard was too weak to even speak and passed out. The

WITNESS TO HISTORY

John Pritchard was Manitoba's version of *Little Big Man*: a great eyewitness to history who seemed to defy death.

For example, he was one of seven survivors at the Battle of Seven Oaks in 1816, when a North West Company brigade killed 21 of 28 Hudson Bay Company men.

Pritchard had switched from the NWC to HBC years earlier, making him much hated by the North West Company. He lay wounded when Métis Francis Ducharme moved in to deliver the death blow. But Métis leader and NWC man Cuthbert Grant held Ducharme back.

Ten years later, Pritchard's business was destroyed in the Red River flood of 1826, the worst flood in Manitoba recorded history. But Pritchard survived.

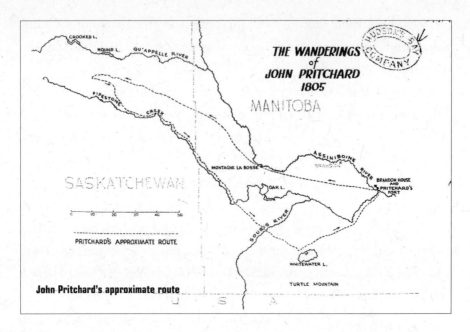

THE WANDERINGS
of
JOHN PRITCHARD
1805

John Pritchard's approximate route

boys were with their family and the family gave him pemmican and water, then transported him to a nearby aboriginal settlement of about 40 teepees, which Ritchie said is approximately where Boissevain is today.

"They would have recognized him as one of the fur traders they dealt with," said Ritchie. Then the Sioux made a seven-day, 100-kilometre trek along the Mandan Trail. They transported him on a sled-like device called a travois that is dragged behind a horse. Finally, they delivered Pritchard to Fort La Souris, from where his misadventure began.

Later that year, Assiniboine Sioux would slaughter a party of independent fur traders along the Souris River. Yet their extraordinary act of kindness toward Pritchard is not unusual for aboriginal people throughout history, said Ritchie.

"I think that kind of generosity is part of the morality of aboriginal people, both then and now. I think if you ask any natives [about the Sioux rescue of Pritchard], they wouldn't be surprised by how the family responded."

The Assiniboine Sioux later moved west, and most are located in Saskatchewan today.

We followed Highway 346, which loosely follows the old Mandan Trail, to near Treesbank. There, Pritchard was nursed back to health, and was visited by his sheepish companion, who explained that he couldn't find the campsite again, so continued on to the Qu'Appelle trading post.

Pritchard lived to the ripe old age, especially back then, of 79 years. He would enjoy careers as a politician, businessman, farmer, writer and educator, in addition to fur trader.

It is interesting to note the length of his ordeal on the prairie: 40 days. It has many parallels in the Bible, where 40 days stands for a period of probation and transformation. Jesus Christ spent 40 days solitude in the wilderness. Moses stayed 40 days on the mount where he produced the 10 Commandments. It rained 40 days and nights in the story of Noah's ark.

Even on the TV show *Survivor*, as if not to infringe on the biblical 40 days, it takes 39 days to "outplay, outwit, and outlast."

Special thanks to the late Hal G. Duncan for his story about Pritchard contained in the self-published book, The South-West Corner.

WHO WAS JOHN PRITCHARD?

- He was a fur trader, politician, farmer, author, businessman and teacher.
- Lord Selkirk appointed him colonial councillor of the Red River Settlement in 1815, the equivalent of an MLA today.
- Pritchard operated his own business, Buffalo Wool Company, from 1820-26. It was destroyed in the Red River flood of 1826.
- He wrote *Glimpses of the Past in the Red River Settlement...1805-1836.*
- He taught Sunday school and is believed to have started schools in Middlechurch and East Kildonan that were open to children regardless of their parents' ability to pay.
- He married, an aboriginal woman and they had at least one son, and also Catherine McLean, in 1816, with whom he had nine children.
- Pritchard was born in Shropshire, England, in 1777 and died in 1856 in the Red River Settlement.

Source: Dictionary of Canadian Biography Online

Donkey from Art Martens's farm near Kleefeld

Critters

LOKI REFUSED TO BID GOODBYE TO SUMMER
September 9, 2007

WHITESHELL PROVINCIAL PARK — The cat didn't come back.

A fluke of scheduling had the whole family off on the Tuesday after Labour Day weekend, so we all stayed at the lake the extra day.

This included our cat Loki, whose schedule is pretty flexible. "Loki, will your boss let you have the day off from hiding in the hedges waiting for unsuspecting sparrows to land?"

"Meow," he replied, with that Kleefeld accent of his, which is where he came from.

Staying at the cottage the day after the unofficial end of summer is like the happy ending to a movie. You feel like you've won. The city has gone back

Bill Redekop and son
Ethan try to coax Loki

to the city. The lake is suddenly eerily quiet — eerie because you're not sure you can trust it, like the quiet before a surprise party.

I was out another time on the day after Labour Day and solo canoed down the centre of the lake, as if to reclaim it. It was showing off a bit, maybe, if there was anyone to show off to because the lake was completely still and boat-less and all I saw were some retirees puttering around in their yards. It was quite wonderful: solitude, the whole lake, the melancholy of summer's end.

This year, an onshore wind was pretty strong so we took the 14-footer with the 9.9-horsepower outboard motor instead. It was just me and our five-year-old, who was about to go into Grade 1 and had started counting the days from Day 11 on down.

We boated the lake's circumference. I sat at the back and steered. He ate cheesies. His fingers and mouth soon turned orange, and he cleaned his fingers by sucking on them one by one until every finger was glistening, not unlike a practise of his father's. We saw two kayaks and a canoe so I felt a little guilty about our fume-puffing outboard. But the wind picked up so it was the right decision.

We saw an elderly man with a cane. He stood at the end of the dock. He wore sweat pants and very white runners that didn't look like they'd seen the outdoors before. His younger son, presumably, was cleaning up.

My little abecedarian waved but the elderly man didn't see him. He was gazing off elsewhere, into the past perhaps. But he was also, like us but more so, trying to drink it all in before the end of the season. An impossibility, of course. But at his age, he might not see it again.

When he turned our way, it was by increments. Ah, he saw us. He waved back. Then we watched as he started to walk off the dock. It was the kind of walking where you move one foot slightly forward, then bring the other foot parallel to it, not past it.

"We're the only ones who are not old but out," the abecedarian observed, in his made-up syntax.

He sang a few songs, the sea chanty *I's The B'y,* mixed with Shel Silverstein tunes, *The Unicorn,* and, strangely, *Marie Laveau* — it's uncertain why the abecedarian's favourite song is about a voodoo queen in Louisiana who kills male suitors.

We returned to the cottage and got ready to leave, since we wanted to be ready for school, etc., work, etc., and by mid-afternoon had more or less packed when someone wondered where the cat was. No one had seen him since noon.

The search began. We called out his name. We tinkled a knife against his dish. We looked in all his favourite hiding spots, and looked again. Twice I crawled under the cottage on my back and belly in the dust and dirt and old crispy leaves that should be carbon-dated. Not there.

Then we walked down the road calling his name, the abecedarian tinkling a knife against Loki's dish like the little drummer boy. We weren't self-conscious because no one else was out.

By late afternoon, it seemed like clouds had moved in on a sunny day, when, really, they hadn't. It was just our moods. My wife was starting to say things like, "I don't think we'll ever see Loki again." A fox, or owl, or wolves, or aliens had surely got hold of our pet.

"Bah!" I said. Loki was just hiding somewhere and didn't want to go home. I was in favour of leaving him out and teaching him a lesson. "That cat's playing us like a cheap cigar," I said, unsure whether "cheap cigar" was really the metaphor I was looking for.

By 7 p.m., we started for home without him. I was privately happy. This would teach that cat to ignore our calls. But if the worst had happened...

"Well, curiosity killed the cat," I said on the drive home. "At least he went doing what he loved," (i.e., hunting mice), I added. My wife only made a face each time I uttered these bon mots.

The abecedarian and I drove out the next night after my work and his first day of school. The moral of this story would have been much clearer if we'd returned to find the cat disheveled, with matted fur and a tip of its ear missing, and a look of desperation in his eyes.

But five minutes after we got there, Loki sauntered out of the bush, in no hurry at all, as if he hadn't seen us for, oh, maybe an hour. He came inside, ate only a small portion of his kibbles — he wasn't very hungry — then padded back to the door. He reached up and wrapped his paws around the doorknob. He wanted to go out.

OK, the cat did come back. And after I grabbed him and stuffed him into his cage, he caterwauled all the way back to Winnipeg.

PATCHES THE DOG IS HOME ALONE, BUT NEVER LONELY

January 9, 2006

MILNER RIDGE — The Winnipeg Humane Society was called, and animal control, and finally, the provincial veterinarian.

People called to say how sorry they felt for the poor dog that lived in an abandoned house in a clearing in the woods near Milner Ridge, 75 kilometres east of Winnipeg.

When investigators checked it out, what they found was a dog leading the life of Riley.

Patches, a springer spaniel, has two doghouses, water from an underground spring, three types of dog food that people bring him (in addition to deer scraps from hunters), an old shack for shelter, dense woods where he catches bush rabbits, and a community that loves him.

Patches lives here. He's lived here alone ever since a family pulled up stakes and abandoned him and the house six years ago.

"If we have a steak dinner, we always leave a little meat on the bones for Patches," said Ernie Okrainec, who drops off food every Sunday, and brought 12 bales of flax straw to make a bed for Patches.

Okrainec also brings treats on special occasions like Thanksgiving and Christmas.

It's a community effort.

Different people drop off food and water on other days. One couple in the area brings entire cooked dinners like fried liver, and the husband brings Patches cheeseburgers from a food stand at Seddons Corner on his way home from work.

People decorate the dog's yard at Christmas and Halloween.

Patches can often be spotted on a pile of logs in the yard watching cars go by, or sleeping. Someone decided to build him a doghouse and placed it on the logs. Patches sometimes sleeps on top of the doghouse, à la Snoopy, but won't go inside.

Ernie Okrainec with Patches

So, someone built him a bigger doghouse. That didn't fly either.

The doghouses now serve as pantries: deer scraps go in the smaller one, and dog food kernels in the larger one. The larger doghouse has three dishes with a different variety of dried dog food in each.

When you visit Patches, it feels like you're on his property. Yellow-stained snow lines the top of the unshovelled driveway, like a gate. On our first visit with neighbour Brian Zolinski, Patches trotted out cautiously from the house to check the guests. Patches also walked us to the highway when it was time to leave. (Or maybe it was his way of hinting it was time we left!)

But it also feels weird: a dog and an empty house.

He's a beautiful dog. He lowers his head and looks up at you with sweet eyes, masked with black patches. The only explanation evolution could have for a springer spaniel's black-and-white markings is camouflage for sleeping on a patchwork quilt.

Patches isn't a barker either, and no one has ever complained about him. His long hair protects him in winter. When it gets really cold, he goes under the house or into a shack in back.

People have tried to adopt him. A well-intentioned family from Lac du Bonnet loaded him up in their vehicle once and started driving down the highway. Patches went crazy, tearing apart their van. They quickly brought him back. Another family from Beausejour tried the same thing, with the same results.

"He would have just come back anyway," said Okrainec.

To hear people talk, Patches belongs with the Savage Sams, Big Reds, Call of the Wilds, even the B-I-N-G-Os of children's books and songs.

Patches does some hunting, too — his breed is traditionally a sporting dog used for finding and flushing out game. "I saw some blood on his nose and I thought, 'What the heck? Was he in a fight?'" Okrainec recalled. "Here it was he'd caught a bush rabbit. My wife said she wouldn't be surprised if he had a deer hanging in the bush."

Patches has almost certainly encountered wolves, considering his postal code is the edge of Agassiz Provincial Forest. Okrainec thinks he had a run-in with a bear once. "What happened to you, boy?" Okrainec said, when he saw a piece of flesh the size of a bear paw torn out of his back. A cloud of flies hovered around, trying to lay eggs in the wound.

Okrainec drove back to Lac du Bonnet, got some salve and tick powder, and treated Patches until his wound completely healed.

Okrainec, 67, became a bit misty-eyed talking about it. He's a softy. His own springer spaniel passed away about four years ago, so Okrainec knows the breed and how attached the dogs become to a single master and place. He didn't get another pet dog because he worried what would happen if he suddenly couldn't care for it anymore.

Ernie and his wife — whose name is "Leave me out of this," she said, when asked — have stacks of photographs of Patches, including a framed picture for the mantle.

Okrainec even has two bobble-head dog dolls on his dashboard. When Okrainec drives up in his van, Patches comes tearing up a path of the long country driveway, and is at the van door before Ernie rolls to a stop.

Patches has also left a legacy. About a year ago, a female dog of a different breed, who lives about five kilometres down the road, had a litter of eight pups. The pups all looked like Patches.

"The owner doesn't know how he did it. She says she keeps her dog tied up all the time," Okrainec said.

There is a dog catcher in the area who gets paid $75 per dog, but local people had a little confab with him years ago concerning Patches. "The dog isn't bothering anyone," maintained Marlene Watson, chief administrator for the RM of Lac du Bonnet.

The community is protective of Patches. People either don't know or won't say who owns the land where Patches lives, even the municipal office. It seems to be provincial land, part of Agassiz Provincial Forest. In the 1960s, a lot of squatters lived on adjacent land.

People were concerned that writing about Patches would prompt a humane society to take him away. Vickie Burns, executive director of the Winnipeg Humane Society, said they don't have to worry.

She looked into the case of Patches years ago. Because Patches lives outside the humane society's Winnipeg jurisdiction, Burns called the provincial veterinarian to investigate. The vet looked into it, took some photos, and came to the conclusion that Patches is one lucky dog.

"The dog is being cared for. It would be cruel to take it away," said Burns. "There's no point in us picking up an animal just to euthanize it."

Just six months later came sad news. Patches died of cancer.

He'd lived alone for seven years. He was 11 years old.

His original family phoned me to say they still visited Patches when he was alive. Serious family strife, and the fact that Patches was not a dog that could be tied down in a backyard in town, prevented the owners from taking Patches with them when they moved. So the entire community had adopted the pooch.

"I just want to say thank you to everybody who fed Patches, and to the people who built the houses," said the family member, who did not wish to be named.

Patches contracted cancer of the mouth, which quickly moved into his throat and made it very difficult for him to eat, a vet hired by Okrainec determined.

It became obvious that Patches was in increasing pain in recent weeks, and he would cry out when he tried to run because the cancer had spread to his lungs.

A veterinarian euthanized Patches and he was buried beside the house he refused to leave.

The original owners placed flowers on his grave, and an anonymous visitor placed flowers by his doghouse.

HE DOES THE BISON BOOGIE
July 12, 2010

NEAR ROBLIN — He rides them, dances with them, even lets the bison roam inside his house.

And Henry Makinson, who has a relationship with bison unlike anyone else, offers this little secret about the beasts: they love having their armpits rubbed. They almost go into a trance.

If bison rancher Makinson had an aboriginal name, it might be Dances with Bison.

OK, they don't exactly dance cheek to cheek. It's more like a conga line. Makinson kneels down and the bison puts its hooves on his back. As it's doing that, Makinson stands up. Then they hokey pokey along, the bison on its back hooves.

In Arborg once, as entertainment at the local rodeo, pet bison Sweet Pea put its hooves on Makinson before he was ready and trampled him. The crowd looked on in horror. But Makinson was OK, got up, coaxed Sweet Pea into putting its hooves on his back again and they did their conga-line routine to the roar of the crowd.

Makinson has been ranching bison for two decades. He refers to the livestock by the colloquial name, buffalo, even though bison is more technically correct.

Makinson's 80 years old now and has suffered some injuries recently. So when I saw him trying to jump on the back of a bison named Patrick to make a better photograph, I heard myself shouting, "No! No!" He stopped.

Bison are the largest land animal in North America, reaching up to 1,360 kg (3,000 lb). They're ornery, short-tempered and excitable — and have horns that can impale you. Other bison ranchers, said Makinson, "think I'm crazy, because a buffalo will kill you."

But to be with Makinson when he mingles among the bison is one of the most extraordinary experiences. We were outside his pickup truck surrounded by the most beautiful bison imaginable, with their giant heads and giant eyes looking at you shyly. The coats and colouring of his bison are so

Henry Makinson with pet bison, Patrick

rich and dark and healthy.

You get a sample of their power when one of them butted the back of the pickup, causing it to lurch. They seem to change attitudes quickly. "If the tail goes up, you better be running," Makinson said. One bison's tail kept rising to half mast. "You have to watch that one," he said.

Makinson believes he still holds the North American record for highest-priced female bison. He sold the female to a buyer in Wyoming for $48,000 — his animals are simply that gorgeous. A good price is considered $8,000 to $10,000.

He lets the bison into his one-room farmhouse that he keeps in addition to his main house in town. It's partly how they become pets. If a bison is born in extreme cold or seems sickly, Makinson has taken the newborn — if the mother allows it — into his house to dry off. He will bottle feed it if necessary.

He lets the tamer, full-grown bison into his house, too, and even into his good house in the southwest corner of Roblin. "They hate walking on linoleum. But Cathy [another pet bison] will get in my living room with the carpeting and she doesn't want to leave. She just wants to lie down and snooze," he said.

"Cathy still walks in the house. She comes in and looks in the mirror and starts talking. She starts grunting, but the buffalo in the mirror's not answering."

One of Makinson's tricks is to lie on the ground and play dead. Cathy will try to roll him over with her head.

His farm is about halfway between Grandview and Roblin, about 375 kilometres northwest of Winnipeg. He's hosted visitors on his farm from as far away as Peru, Germany, Austria, Ukraine and Japan, as well as from the United States. Some priests from Ukraine visited and shot video of him riding a bison.

Makinson's father was from the Orkney Islands and his mother was third- generation Ukrainian-Canadian.

He was injured last year while loading the bison because someone left an in-gate open and he was trampled. And this winter, while feeding the bison, one named Patrick butted him gently to push him away and its horn caught under Makinson's snowmobile suit belt. "He lifted his head and lifted me up. He was carrying me. He was backing up and I was dangling from his horn."

It hurt his back but he says he's mostly recovered now.

ATTACK OF THE KILLER DONKEYS
March 4, 2003

KLEEFELD — So what does Art Martens do with all those donkeys he raises anyway?

Milk 'em? Shave 'em? Fatten 'em?

No, he rents them out as guard donkeys.

Martens rents guard donkeys to ranchers in Manitoba's growing cattle industry. While cattle numbers are increasing by leaps and bounds, so are coyote and timber wolf populations.

Donkeys, as it turns out, have a violent dislike for dogs.

"They hate dogs. Dogs just make them ornery. They have a sense that dogs are no good," explained Martens.

A donkey will catch a wild dog in its teeth and stomp it to death, he said.

Martens maintains donkeys can run even faster than horses — when the mood strikes them, and the mood strikes them when it comes to wolves and coyotes. At full speed, a donkey can kick out a sharp hoof in any direction at whatever it's chasing.

"I've had complaints from farmers who say the donkey just stands in their field and doesn't move. But when it's time to move, they really move," said Martens.

Art Martens and his donkeys

"The donkey integrates into a herd of cattle and that herd then becomes theirs. So they protect it."

And donkeys do live up to stereotype.

"Oh, they're stubborn. They're so stubborn," said Martens, 48. "You have to have patience. We've learned not to chase them into the chute. We don't try to drag them around any more. You can't halter them and lead them around like a horse. They just dig their little feet into the ground and you can't budge them."

Martens started his donkey rental business three years ago from his ranch near Kleefeld, about 50 kilometres south of Winnipeg. He puts up with more than the occasional quip that his place is where the jackasses hang out. Jacks are male asses and jennies are the females.

He has 19 donkeys, and will have about 30 by spring. He and wife Carol are thinking of having a sign made. "We're probably going to call this place Kicking Ass Ranch," he said.

Martens also sells the donkeys, but it's easier for most farmers to just rent them from spring to fall. Just the cost of trimming their hooves twice a year would cost the farmer $100. That's included in the $300 per season that Martens rents the animals for.

He got into the business as a farrier, a person who trims horses' hooves that otherwise grow too long and crack and curve until the horse turns lame. Martens got into being a farrier because his kids belonged to 4-H and were into horses. So they raised some horses on their 40-acre farm.

Donkeys have the same problem with their hooves as horses, so Martens combined his skill as a farrier with a market niche. He has stopped trimming horse hooves. "Farriers don't last long because their backs give out," Martens said.

Renting donkeys is just a sideline. His full-time job is as a trucker. He also raises six heifers each year, which he butchers and then sells locally.

He is the only donkey breeder in the province with a herd of any size, as far as he knows.

Donkeys will even fight a bear that threatens the herd. Martens knows of a donkey near Vita that had to be stitched up after it fought off a bear.

Their brays can be very noisy. "That's part of their defence. If there's something in the fence that's not supposed to be there, their yelling turns vicious," he said.

"They also have very sharp ears. Their sense of hearing is unreal. I step out the door on my way to work, and they'll hear me in the pasture a quarter-mile away and start braying."

Grunthal-area farmer Lauren Wiebe said he'd heard of Martens' donkeys and rented two last summer when he had 600 heifers.

"I heard a story that donkeys were natural protectors," Wiebe said. "We thought we'd give it a try."

Wiebe said he was unaware of any coyote attacks on his herd but he once saw a dog wander into the cattle.

"The donkey just went over and separated the dog from the herd," Wiebe said. "The dog was simply gone."

Wiebe said he's convinced the donkeys worked because he didn't lose any cattle last summer, adding he's planning to bring in 1,000 steers this summer and will rent at least two donkeys again.

WE'VE BEEN BUFFALOED;
THOSE THINGS ARE BISON
October 14, 2004

FARGO, N. D. — Great Plains raconteur Tom Isern sat across from me in a diner in Fargo, North Dakota, last spring and gave me such a look.

We were discussing depopulation in North Dakota, and the Buffalo Commons idea of turning the Great Plains into a giant wild-animal park. (Note: Buffalo Commons is an idea proposed in 1987 by Frank J. Popper and Deborah Popper that drier parts of the Great Plains be returned to nature because they are not sustainable.)

Local bison herd

Isern, a North Dakota State University history prof and columnist on Great Plains issues, at one point emphasized the irony that some North Dakota farmers now raise "buffalo."

"Just a minute, Tom," I corrected him. "Technically, they are bison, not buffalo."

What a look he gave me, sitting across the table at the Sons of Norway restaurant. I felt like some high-falutin' Easterner with a derby hat, bolo tie and fob watch, sitting across from cowpoke Isern wearing a metaphoric cowhide vest, speckled neckerchief and cowboy hat which, if he slapped it against his thigh, would give off a cloud of trail dust.

"Whatever," he said impatiently.

Whatever.

And he's right. I'm not sure how long ago it was that it suddenly became a big deal whether you called them bison or buffalo. An expert, I believe a local university biologist, pointed out we'd been wrong all these years in calling them buffalo. They are actually bison.

Buffalo live in India and South Africa. Indian buffalo like to stand up to their necks in water all day, while African or Cape buffalo have a set of horns that look like Annette Funicello's flip hairdo in *Dr. Goldfoot and the Bikini Machine* (1965).

What we have here on the Great Plains are bison.

I'd rather not know that. Buffalo is a lot more fun to say than bison. Buffalo has a nice "fffff" sound in the centre and ends in a vowel like some Italian oratorio. Whereas "bison" has more the ring of sound business advice you get from your dad: "Buy low, sell high, son," which eventually came out as the derivative "Buy-son," which eventually got slanged into "bison."

I mean, bison sounds like an animal that goes to the barber every second week, never snorts and is always well-behaved.

Buffalo sounds like an ornery slob with one shirt flap untucked, who'd as soon gore you with a horn and toss you into the treetops.

A bison stands politely and answers all the media's questions, without ever saying much or offending anyone.

A buffalo answers every question ironically, or answers every question with a question, and doesn't care what the media write about it because we're all pond scum anyway and we'll write whatever we feel like writing.

My point is, the word buffalo is a colloquialism — a word or expression grown out of regional dialect — decided by our forbears.

For whatever reason, maybe ignorance, but not necessarily — we don't know that — our forbears started to call them "buffalo."

Maybe they wanted to colour it up a bit when writing back to Europe. Or maybe Bison Bill just doesn't conjure up the same showmanship.

Regardless, it was completely democratic. No one forced them to say buffalo instead of bison. I accept their common will to warp and twist the language as they felt like it. It's called heritage. And it wouldn't be the first time we named something wrong, would it, Christopher Columbus?

I think we're too gullible about sentences that begin with "researchers say," or end with "according to experts." I also have this nagging feeling we in Manitoba will eventually be browbeaten because we call our best eating fish a pickerel, while the rest of the world calls it a walleye.

I have this fear that someone out there is about to tell us that no, they're not pickerel, real pickerel are actually little speckled warblers that makes their habitat in the Chilean mountains and poop in the wine there, giving it its unique taste.

The buffalo nearly went extinct once. Let's not let it happen again.

From the Committee to Save the Buffalo From Experts.

FOWLS MORE THAN FAIR AT CATCHING FLIES
July 17, 2005

MANITOU — Snap… Snap… Snap.

Another one bites the dust.

And another fly gone and another fly gone….

Enough with the Queen. The snap of a Muscovy duck's bill on another

Muscovy ducks

fly is a sweet enough sound on a Manitoba farm on a summer afternoon. That's because the strange ducks, imported from Brazil, feast on flies. Black flies. House flies. Blue bottle, deer and horse flies.

"Man, do they eat up flies," said Ewald Matthys, a sheep producer near Manitou, about 150 kilometres southwest of Winnipeg, who purchased his first Muscovies four years ago. Matthys is one of a handful of farmers using the ducks to rid themselves of the pesky insects.

"In my yard, it used to be black with flies," said Matthys, who keeps about 60 sheep. "Now, I have no problem."

There is still the odd fly in Matthys's barn but not the swarms there used to be. Barns are normally the O'Hare airports of the fly kingdom.

Watching the Muscovy ducks snare black flies out of mid-air is a bit of poetry in motion. The Muscovies will hunker down and remain completely still, then suddenly arch out their necks and... snap.

The evidence is not just anecdotal. A University of Guelph study found Muscovy ducks remove 30 times more flies than traditional fly paper in dairy barns and pig pens. (Farmers use industrial-strength fly paper that comes in sheets about ⅓ metre by 3 metres that are tacked to barn walls and beams.)

In one pen, a single Muscovy duck reduced adult fly numbers by 97 per cent, according to the study. In two dairy enclosures, Muscovies reduced the fly population by 84 and 93 per cent respectively.

They know their prey. Flies like to hang out around dung. So Muscovies will linger over fresh piles of dung, shagging flies out of the air like right fielders. Once they've got the air traffic under control, they will dig out the fly eggs and maggots nested in the dung.

Matthys has five adult Muscovies and six chicks. It's more than he needs. He says the ducks are so voracious he doesn't need more than his original four ducks to clear his entire farmyard.

Matthys also keeps guinea hens, known for their ability to forage for ticks.

"They go out in the yard four times a day and pick up nothing but wood ticks," Matthys said. The hens are used extensively in the United States to combat deer ticks, which can carry lyme disease.

Matthys also has a Jack Russell terrier, a dog not much bigger than a poodle — too small, one would think, for a farm. Yet it is the dog's genetic forte to hunt down and kill rats.

"We'll be driving along on my tractor and he'll spot something in the grass, and he jumps out after it," said Matthys, 65.

Muscovy ducks come in a variety of colours. All have red crests across their eyes like bandits, but farmers will vouch these are the good guys.

Farmers have been snapping up Muscovy ducks for years, said Karin Bannister, who operates nearby Granny's Miniature Farm, where she keeps Muscovies, among many other exotic farm animals, or "critters," as she calls them.

One might say the Muscovies take to Manitoba like ducks to water, except these ducks hate water, said Bannister. Muscovies don't have oil on their feathers to protect them from being waterlogged the way most ducks do.

Muscovies are peaceful and easy to raise, and get along well with other barn-yard animals. And they are a relatively quiet animal — they don't quack. Instead, they hiss. "That's just their way of talking to each other," Bannister said.

Barn swallows also like a diet of flies, as do Japanese quail, she added. Muscovies eat mosquitoes, too, but not nearly enough.

Ewald Matthys watches his Muscovy ducks shag flies

International aid agencies use Muscovy ducks in many developing countries to control locusts in addition to flies.

Matthys doesn't have to cage the birds. They hang around the barn because that's where there is food and fresh drinking water. They also eat grass and other vegetation. They can fly, but not very well, and only about a metre off the ground.

Muscovies are supposed to be tasty eating when they get too slow to pick off the little buzzers. But Matthys says no thanks, after watching them forage in dung piles all day.

One drawback to Muscovies is they produce a lot of manure themselves, perhaps as some evolutionary trait to attract their flying dinners.

There are a variety of places to purchase Muscovies, one of them being through members of the Manitoba Quack and Cluck Club, which holds regular auctions and yard sales. The club can be found on the Internet.

THEY ROAM ON THE RANGE
April 17, 2010

CHITEK LAKE — Oh, give me a home, where the buffalo roam...

In 1991, the Manitoba government did just that.

Except it wasn't a home where the buffalo roam, like in the old song. It was a home where the buffalo could roam.

That year, Manitoba Conservation released 13 wood bison into the unorganized territories of North Interlake, between lakes Winnipeg and Winnipegosis.

No borders. No fences. Just go. You're free.

And go they did. With virtually no help from humans, other than blocks of salt that Manitoba Conservation would drop off to ensure they had enough minerals in their diet, the bison not only survived but began to reproduce.

In 1996, Manitoba Conservation released nine more wood bison.

It's quite a trek to see the results of that release, now almost 20 years later. On our trip up to Chitek Lake, photographer Boris Minkevich and I travelled four hours by car on Highway 6; another hour by bombardier through 35 kilometres of bush; and 45 minutes by snowmobile, to reach the bison release point.

We went up in early March, which is why you see snow in Boris's photos. The terrain is so marshy that winter is the best — almost the only — time to see the wood bison. In summer, it takes 12 to 14 hours to reach here by quad, and that's just from Highway 6.

After such a long trip, we half expected a greeting party of bison, perhaps even hostesses with hors d'oeuvres trays. It quickly became apparent this wasn't going to be like spotting bison in a national park. We would have to search for these animals, travelling the lake on snowmobiles. Chitek is a large lake, about 15 kilometres long and 10 kilometres wide.

They were out there, though. Great fields of bison scat told us that, easy to spot against the lake's snowy surface. Even the scat of these giant beasts is impressive: dark leathery piles as large as tree stumps in some cases. The wood bison is North America's largest land mammal, almost 15 per cent larger than the plains bison, with bulls weighing up to a tonne.

Bison at Chitek Lake

We saw our first herd a short time later but they saw us first and ske-daddled into the woods. A few straggled behind, eyeing us warily, before they bolted, too.

It's something to see a bison at full gallop. They spring off all fours like a mule deer, all four hooves airborne at once. You almost expect their limbs, resembling stick legs, to snap under the weight of their massive torsos. Yet they can really move.

"The first couple of years [after release] you could drive right up beside them. They're getting wilder and wilder," observed Gord Kirbyson, our guide and a Manitoba natural resource officer based in Gypsumville.

A little later, we found a wolf kill from the previous week. Some bison yearlings had been playing on a beaver lodge when one fell through the thin ice over the beaver hole and couldn't get out.

Wolves found it and cleaned it up almost immaculately. It was like they'd wiped a plate clean with a hunk of bread. All that remained was the bison robe. Not even a bone was left over. The wolves grind up the bone for the marrow inside. We were definitely in the wilderness now.

"I've read literature that says it can sometimes take wolves 20 years before they learn how to make a kill on bison," said Brian Joynt, our other guide and Manitoba Conservation wildlife manager for the central region based in Gimli. Which suggests there will be more bison kills in the future, especially with the wolf population as high as it is.

We were starting to lose daylight and worried we wouldn't get photos, although our guides didn't seem concerned. We stopped at a vacant shack called the Super 8 where some ice fishermen from Skownan First Nation bed down during the commercial fishing season. It's called the Super 8 because legend has it that eight fishermen once managed to sleep in there at one time.

Chitek Lake is stocked with pickerel, and 22 families of commercial fishers from Skownan work it. They gross an average of about $60,000 each from a month's fishing, and there are other lakes they net fish in the area, too.

The bison will sometimes congregate around the lake's handful of fishing cabins like the Super 8 to feed, but not today. "That's why fishermen like the bison so much. It's a unique feeling to get up in the morning and have 10 bison standing on your doorstep," said Joynt.

It was going on 5 p.m. when lead snowmobiler Kirbyson stopped and we all stopped in formation and looked to where he pointed out a herd of bison. We moved cautiously nearer for a better look. What magnificent creatures they are.

The herd numbered 30 to 40. They didn't run this time but stood and watched us, albeit warily and a bit grumpily. They do that bovine stand-and-stare thing. But you have to remember that bison can be catankerous creatures, not docile like cattle. What are the differences between wood and plains bison? Woods are bigger, taller, slimmer, darker and, surprisingly, not as hairy. Their cape, that furry front half, is less pronounced than that of plains bison.

The surest way to tell the difference between the two is that the wood bison's hump is well ahead of its front legs. The plains bison hump is less pronounced and directly over the front legs.

The wood's head hair is straighter, too, and sometimes falls into its eyes; the plains bison's hair is nearly an Afro and stacks on its head. Straighter hair can make it look as if the wood bison's horns are longer, but they aren't. Some of the wood bison we saw almost looked like Texas Longhorns, with long, curly, pointy horns.

When we went out again the following morning, we saw bison playing, head-butting and pushing each other around.

For all their girth and power and prehistoric looks, bison are also funny creatures, and the MTS ads pick up on it. Rotund and with beards, Mr. French (actor Sebastian Cabot) of 1960s TV show, *Family Affair*, comes to mind, for both the looks and the easily-bruised dignity.

Also, their massive heads droop low and can't be raised above shoulder level. You could dangle a small toy from a string above their noses and they'd never see it — but tie it to a very long pole if you try this. When one bison stared at me, he peered upwards like a physician looking over reading glasses.

The bison will stick their heads in the snow and swing back and forth to get at the sedge grass underneath. Combined with the condensation from their breath, their faces become encrusted with snow and large ice collars. They'll walk around like that for days, like snow monsters.

So what happened to the 22 bison released into this wilderness area north of Gypsumville? Manitoba Conservation did an aerial survey in 2009. The department counted 212 individuals but estimates there are more like 300 wood bison here today.

* * *

What will happen to these wood bison in the future is uncertain. No one really planned that far ahead. The bison have started to range farther afield, and half a dozen even turned up on Highway 60 near Easterville, north of Chitek. Hitting a bison on a road at night would be like ramming into the Richardson Building.

The original land here was scouted by Dr. Harvey Payne for Manitoba Conservation. It's ideal for wood bison with its aspen, poplar, pine and sedges (grasses in meadows and sloughs). Meadow sedge is the bison's main food, and large sedge flats rim the shoreline of Chitek Lake.

The bison don't seem bothered standing in water either, so long as they can eat. They also swim. They'll swim back and forth across the lake, said Kirbyson, and what a sight that must be. In winter, you'll get the occasional stampede on Chitek Lake, a great cloud of churned up snow moving across the horizon.

The wood bison population for North America never totalled more than 170,000 in the 1800s, not like the estimated 30 to 70 million of plains bison.

But like the plains bison, the wood bison nearly became extinct. It wasn't due to unfettered capitalism but merely increased human occupation in the north and hunting for food with improved technology, like rifles.

Actually, wood bison were believed to have become extinct. Then, in 1957, a small herd was discovered in the Mackenzie Delta in the Northwest Territories.

That herd started a national recovery program. The first wood bison went to the Mackenzie Bison Sanctuary in the NWT.

Skownan First Nation, north of Waterhen, took a small number of the wood bison in 1984 and penned them. They have been tended there by the man people call the "bison whisperer," Raymond Marion of Skownan First Nation.

There was some controversy, however. The Canadian Wildlife Service objected to moving an endangered species outside its natural range. That is, scientific opinion is that the wood bison never inhabited Manitoba. The farthest east wood bison ranged was the very northwest edge of Saskatchewan. So it's a recovery program in Manitoba, not a reintroduction program.

There are Manitobans who contest that view, especially seeing how easily the bison have adapted here. There's a belief the bison once roamed in the Cedar Lake area north of Chitek Lake. But that won't be accepted opinion "until someone finds a wood bison skull carbon-dated back to such and such a time," said Joynt.

Today, the bison in Manitoba are peppered throughout a 2,500 square kilometre area from Waterhen Lake to the south, to Sisib Soul Lake and Pickerel Lake in the north.

The province tried its first wild release from the Skownan herd in 1988. But the bison wandered south into agricultural land, instead of north as handlers hoped. The second time, Manitoba Conservation built a pen on the shore of Chitek Lake. They held the bison there for six weeks to get them acclimatized. It's called a soft release. This time the bison stayed.

"It was part of a national recovery strategy. It was to have four or five different disease-free wild herds in the country," said Joynt.

But a herd in Manitoba makes a lot of sense. Even if Manitoba is not traditional land, this herd is so far apart from the other herds that diseases that plague wood bison, like tuberculosis and brucellosis, shouldn't spread to here. The Manitoba herd helps ensure the animal's survival.

Progeny of that original Mackenzie Delta herd have also been released in northern British Columbia and Alberta, in addition to NWT, in areas considered native to wood bison.

* * *

In the late 1990s, forestry company Repap, now owned by Tolko, flagged this area with the intent of harvesting the timber around Chitek Lake and building an all-weather road. The area has the best stands of harvestable pine in the Interlake. Repap's all-weather road would extend L-shaped from Highway 6 west to Chitek Lake, and from Chitek Lake north to Highway 60.

Chitek means "pelican" in Cree, and nearby Atim Lake means "Dog Lake" in Cree. But the area is regarded as the traditional land of the Saulteaux band, Skownan First Nation, located south of Chitek.

Skownan wanted payment from Repap for any trees harvested and Repap balked. Repap said it already had to pay the province royalties. While Skownan signed forestry deals with Louisiana Pacific to the west of Waterhen, and with Tembec to the east, it didn't with Repap around Chitek Lake. (Deals with Louisiana Pacific and Tembec fell through with the collapse of Canada's forestry industry.)

Then Skownan and Manitoba Conservation petitioned the province and obtained park reserve status for Chitek Lake, halting Repap's forestry plans. The status runs for five years after which Skownan could apply for permanent park status. But when five years passed, Skownan didn't apply.

So park reserve status was slapped on again and then expired again. The area is now under its third five-year park reserve status, and there are concerns the area may lose its protection, which may threaten the bison.

Joynt and Kirbyson don't take the same view of forestry as typical environmental lobby groups. The Manitoba Conservation officials aren't so concerned about cutting down trees. The mature trees are falling down now anyway. If they'd been harvested a decade ago when Repap wanted to, new trees would be half grown by now, and harvested forests often result in an explosion of wildlife.

What scares the conservation officials is Repap's proposed all-weather road and logging roads that would branch off it. That invites hunters and they can't be kept out anymore, not with so many driving quads. Put up a blockade and a quad will just go around it. Few things decimate wildlife populations today like roads, said Joynt and Kirbyson.

A permanent park would protect the bison but also other wildlife. Chitek Lake is the only place in Manitoba where you find the four ungulates (hoofed animals) elk, moose, white-tailed deer and woodland caribou. Throw in a fifth ungulate in the wood bison and you have a woodland of international significance.

Skownan Chief Harvey Nepinak is concerned that permanent park status may limit his band's economic opportunities for the area, including hunting, trapping, fishing and forestry.

He made it clear that the wood bison project was to help the animal's recovery but also to provide economic benefits for Skownan. "We want a shared management agreement on the use of these surplus animals," he said. "The province and band need to work out a management plan."

Nepinak would like to see some eco-tourism established for the area, as well as a controlled hunt for wayward bison — a hunt at the edges of the bison range when their numbers grow too large. Some of the other wild bison herds have controlled hunting, like the one at Mackenzie Bison Sanctuary.

Manitoba Conservation doesn't believe the area can support more than 400 bison. At that point, the animals could degrade their habitat to their own detriment. Eat themselves out of house and home, in other words. Also, they could start to range into areas where they would endanger people and themselves.

Joynt agrees that a policy to deal with bison expansion and related issues will need to be developed, possibly sooner rather than later.

"Eventually, we're going to have an issue with the bison and we'll need a policy for wayward animals," Joynt said.

The Free Press would like to thank Manitoba Conservation and employees Brian Joynt and Gord Kirbyson for their time and effort in allowing the newspaper to view the free-ranging wood bison.

Rural Enterprise

PAY IS LOW, COMMITMENT IS HIGH
January 6, 2008

LETELLIER — Their pay is minimal, if anything at all. Their hearts are huge.

And if you should be involved in a collision on one of Manitoba's highways, chances are they will be the first people on the scene to help.

They are members of rural volunteer fire departments, but the name is increasingly a misnomer. Many volunteer fire departments handle more motor vehicle collisions than fires today.

Letellier and District Volunteer Fire Department

Take the members of the Letellier and District Volunteer Fire Department next to busy Highway 75. Their pagers go off up to 15 times a year to attend crashes, often in the dead of night.

The Letellier volunteers race to the fire hall, dress and are out the door in five to eight minutes. In about 85 per cent of cases, they are first on the scene.

"You're always worried about who you will find there," said Gloria Gallant, who has been a volunteer for eight years. "The first thing you think of is whether anyone in your family or a friend was going to be on the road at that time."

Volunteer fire departments perform rescues on highways in every corner of the province, said provincial fire chief Doug Popowich. "We're seeing a big shift," he said. The reason is more traffic — and better fire prevention.

"As you travel along No. 1 Highway, you're going to go through Headingley, which is a volunteer fire department, and Elie, which is a volunteer fire department, Portage is a combination department (full-time and on-call members), and past Portage you hit MacGregor, Austin, Carberry, they're all volunteer departments. And on the other side of Brandon, which has a career fire department, you're going to hit Oak Lake and Virden, and they have volunteer departments," Popowich said.

"And it's the same when you travel north up No. 6 to Thompson."

Letellier's force is still made up strictly of volunteers but most rural fire departments now pay members on a per-call basis. Remuneration depends on a municipality's ability to pay, ranging from $7 to $16 an hour. "The fire departments provide the same level of service as career fire departments do in the city at a fraction of the cost," Popowich said.

A few years ago, pagers started going off at a baseball tournament the local fire department had organized in Letellier. All 25 volunteers left their positions on the baseball diamond to make a rescue.

"That's the commitment level they all give," Popowich said.

The Rural Municipality of Montcalm in southern Manitoba has two volunteer fire departments, one at Letellier, just north of Emerson, and in St. Jean Baptiste.

Of the 25 volunteers in the Letellier fire department, about 15 live in Letellier. Another 54 residents are former volunteers, out of a town of about 200 people. Up to a dozen of the volunteer members at a time have been women.

It's a big part of rural life.

"In the city, you assume someone else will look after those things. Here, you have to think that someone may be sitting in that vehicle down the road bleeding to death," said volunteer Rick Gallant, proprietor of Gallant's Family Foods in Letellier.

The scenes can be grisly.

The first thing volunteers do is reroute traffic. They prioritize which accident victims need help the most. Volunteers will control an injured person's bleeding or start oxygen until an ambulance arrives. They will move individuals if needed.

The Letellier department has its own Jaws of Life for extricating people from wreckage. Rick Gallant has seen Marcel Bissonnette, Letellier's volunteer fire chief for the past 20 years, crawl through the rear window of a smashed-up vehicle to stabilize a patient.

Volunteers also assist paramedics with cardiopulmonary resuscitation on the way to the hospital. "CPR in the back of a moving vehicle is not easy to do. It's better with two people," Bissonnette said.

Their 25-kilometre stretch on Highway 75, starting at the border, keeps them especially busy.

The volunteers rescued former MLA Jack Penner's wife Dora when she was thrown from her snowmobile several years ago. But the ambulance had became stuck trying to reach her, so rescuers had to go in by snowmobile. The Penners donated a snowmobile sled to the Letellier service as a way of saying thanks.

"The hardest ones are when there are kids involved," Bissonnette said. Like on November 11, when three local kids were involved in a rollover. One had a broken neck and another a cracked vertebra.

Had the individual with the broken neck not been moved properly by the volunteer fire department, he would be a paraplegic today. Instead, he is already walking around and all the kids are expected to recover.

There are training requirements for the fire departments, of course. Four members at Letellier, including Bissonnette and Gloria Gallant, have first responder status — 120 hours of training that brings them almost to the level of a starting paramedic.

However, it's not only car crashes and fires they attend.

Luc Chouinard used his CPR training a decade ago when a neighbour's little girl went missing. They found her floating face down in an old cistern. She had clambered onto the lid and fallen in, then the lid had closed behind her.

The little girl was covered in raw sewage, but Chouinard's only thought was his CPR training. Within a minute, the girl's lungs started to kick in.

That girl is now a teenager.

"It's nice to see her today and see that twinkle in her eyes," Chouinard said.

VOLUNTEER FIRE DEPARTMENTS

- There are 213 fire departments in Manitoba. Of those, only Winnipeg and Brandon have entirely full-time paid staff.
- Some fire departments, like in Portage la Prairie and Thompson, are a mix of full-time and on-call staff. The rest are rural fire departments operated by people paid on an on-call basis, or by volunteers.
- From 4,500 to 5,000 people help the fire departments either as volunteers or are paid on an on-call basis.
- Manitoba Public Insurance pays $600 for a motor vehicle accident attended by a rural fire department. The payment rises to $800 if the collision is a complex one requiring, for example, use of the Jaws of Life.
- The MPI payment goes to the municipality with the fire department that attended the collision. The payment is in part because drivers in collisions are not usually from the local community. Rural municipalities tend to reinvest the money into equipment.

MANITOBA COUPLE TRANSFORMS THE LIVES OF ABORIGINAL SIBLINGS

January 7, 2007

ONANOLE — Wayne and Florence Foster have so many kids, dinner is like eating at a Hutterite colony, says Wayne.

For Christmas, the Fosters go through a 40-pound turkey. It takes until lunch for the kids to open all their Christmas presents, which they do by taking turns unwrapping one present at a time.

As for the family surname Foster, well, rarely has a couple been so appropriately named.

Wayne and Florence have nine aboriginal foster children — six girls and three boys — all from the same birth mother. They also have four dogs, a rabbit and a hamster.

And they have an idyllic life. Can someone see a TV series in this?

Six years ago, the *Free Press* reported on the Fosters and their decision to become foster parents to eight aboriginal children from Dakota Plains First Nation. The occasion was a press conference hosted by Dakota Plains to announce it had built a house on the reserve for the Fosters to raise the kids.

It was a great story, but what happened after that? Did that arrangement work? Or did their good intentions fold when reality set in?

A pastel red sunset accompanied the drive to Wayne and Florence Foster's log home on the southern slope of Riding Mountain, near Onanole. It was one of those enchanting winter evenings where the temperature actually rises through the night instead of falling, as if the spin of the Earth had pitched into reverse.

Wayne, a journeyman carpenter, moved the family in 2003 to this partly forested acreage when he built their dream home: a 3,500 square-foot, seven-bedroom pine-log structure.

It's the only way to raise so many kids, he said. "How would you have control of these kids in the city?"

Florence and Wayne Foster with their nine adopted children (from left): Devin, Kyla, Cassie, Corey, Joseph, Jocelyn, Alyssa, Jodie and Natasha

The foster kids were wild and lacking in manners at first, although that's not something the parents like to discuss. Sweethearts is a word that comes to mind now. The children have responded to the parents' love and discipline like plants to sunlight.

"It's pretty impressive," said Dale Wallis, a neighbour in the area who manages nearby Elkhorn Resort, and who drives his snowmobile past the Foster house on his way to Onanole to pick up mail. The community seems to take pride in the Foster foster kids.

"They don't have behaviour issues," Wallis said of the kids. "It's really a matter of those kids knowing they are with family and knowing they are loved. The parents show them love and respect, and it shows."

And discipline. When one of the girls got caught shoplifting, she was grounded for six months. Wayne grew up in the school of hard knocks and doesn't fool around. He's from a foster home himself, ran away at age 13 and has fended for himself ever since. When the *Free Press* article about the Fosters first appeared in 2001, a reader e-mailed the newspaper to say he knew Foster years ago and couldn't think of a finer man to raise the foster children.

By the way, that girl who was grounded is doing amazing things today.

Jodie is a member of the cadets out of Brandon, and has travelled to the Yukon twice in that capacity. She hopes to go to England on a cadet exchange program in two years, and her long-term goal is to become an army nurse.

"When we first moved out here, we didn't know how people would react to us. You'd be amazed. Everyone here just loves these kids to death," said Wayne.

The kids are Devin, age 6, Kyla, 7, Cassie, 8, Corey, 9, Joseph, 10, Jocelyn, 12, Alyssa, 13, Jodie, 15, and Natasha, 16.

"They're very caring, loving kids. They help other kids, too," said Flo.

Devin, the youngest, joined the family only four months ago. He'd bounced around from foster home to foster home and Wayne and Flo couldn't bear it anymore. "He was going to grow up thinking nobody loved him enough to take him," said Flo. When she said this, her voice rose in a long arcing inflection like a big heartfelt, Awww!

How the couple began foster parenting bears repeating. Dakota Plains placed an ad in a newspaper seeking foster parents for the children so brothers and sisters could stay together.

Flo heard about the ad and started to get all soft and mushy on Wayne. Wayne and Flo were already in their late 40s at the time, and each had raised two kids in previous marriages.

"I don't think soooo!" was Wayne's response. "My kids were grown up and I was ready to spend my time hunting and fishing," he said. (Even today, most of the meat the family eats is wild game shot by Wayne.)

But Flo couldn't get it out of her head, and probably more so, her heart. "My grandma once told me I should have had 12 children," she said. "I've baby-sat all my life, starting when I was eight years old. I've always had kids around me."

So "just giving it a try" became three children, and "wouldn't it be nice if..." boosted it to six children, which gave way to "what's two more," totalling eight.

And, finally, came Devin, number nine. It was Devin who opened the front door, introduced himself, and showed the visitor the place where he stores his coat and boots — in the hall, where all the kids have their names on masking tape above individual coat hooks. Organization.

Either the seventh or eighth foster child was Kyla. Dakota and Ojibway Child and Family Services asked if the Fosters would mind picking up Kyla in Winnipeg and caring for her for a few weeks until a home could be found. The Fosters could see where this was leading and resisted, but finally agreed.

"Well, our hearts just melted to see this beautiful girl. She was the most gorgeous baby we'd ever seen," said Flo.

"Flo says everything's meant to be," added Wayne.

For Florence and Wayne, it's having patience day in and day out on three hours sleep, especially when the kids were younger.

It means having two freezers, two 80-gallon hot water tanks, and soon, a third fridge.

They racked up 280,000 kilometres on their van the first three years chaperoning the kids around. Nothing was close to the Dakota Plains reserve. The kids have taken voice lessons, judo, swimming, skating, attended bible camp, Sunday school and have been baptized.

During those early days, the family took a 15-day trip to Saskatchewan in a motorhome. "Most of those kids had never seen a beach before. I tell you, it was a trip from hell but it was worth it," said Wayne.

Some of the kids come with issues. Repetition is important. "The main thing is structure, routine, discipline. Children love discipline, although they may not show it," said Flo.

"It's tough love. Whatever you want to call it. Respecting elders. Not talking back," said Wayne.

The family bond between brothers and sisters has helped, although it's hard to measure and even describe. "You can see the kids are always happy," said Flo, and, yes, that's very apparent after three hours.

The family keeps in contact with some aboriginal culture, like attending pow-wows. Wayne and Florence lived as common-law partners initially. At their wedding a few years ago, the children were all decked out in formal aboriginal dress, including jingle dresses for the girls, sans the jingles.

The two oldest girls have part-time jobs. Natasha has been working in a local jewelry shop for three years. Jodie is working at The Spot restaurant, which the family leased the past year so their kids could gain some entry-level work experience.

There is a shortage of foster parents in Manitoba. That's despite an increase in non-aboriginal foster parents of aboriginal children. The increase in foster aboriginal children has been greater. Larger numbers of aboriginal children went into foster homes starting in the 1980s when the province began to halt adoptions of aboriginal children by non-aboriginal people. This decision followed an inquiry by Chief Judge Edwin Kimelman of the Provincial Court in which he called such adoptions "cultural genocide." More kids are also being taken into provincial care as professionals become trained in detecting abuse and neglect by parents.

A high number of aboriginal children are being raised by white foster parents in rural Manitoba. This is especially true in rural Eastern Manitoba, from Lorette, through to Richer, and including Steinbach and the surrounding area.

Wayne and Flo recommend foster parenting but acknowledge that some foster parents are left heartbroken if the children are returned to a birth parent. They know a couple who were crushed after they lost their foster children after three years when the birth parent demanded they be returned. Wayne and Flo had assurances that wasn't likely to happen to them, but it's a fear that never leaves them completely.

It's not all roses. "There are days you could catch the first bus leaving the country," said Wayne. But there's tremendous satisfaction, too. "It's rewarding. When you see the progress they make with some TLC [tender loving care]."

The Fosters give high marks to the Brandon office of Dakota Ojibway Child and Family Services. "They're very good. Their support system is great," said Wayne.

Wayne and Flo are paid on a group home rate. Their grocery bill is about $1,000 every two weeks, even though most of the meat is from Wayne's hunting.

They spend about $2,500 each fall to buy new clothes for the school year, and another $1,500 or so for outerwear once winter starts. Christmas can total about $2,000, although that includes a $50 bonus per child from Dakota Ojibway Child and Family Services.

Because their job never stops, DOCFS gives them a weekend off a month when support staff fill in, but the couple rarely go farther than Brandon, if that.

The Fosters are also delighted with the province's very important decision to bump the foster age to 21. Before, kids lost the support at age 18. "Most kids I know at 18 don't know what they want to do in life," said Wayne.

The birth parents have rights to visit and contact the children, but contact has been limited.

"I just want these kids to achieve the best they can in life," said Wayne.

"They talk to people. They make eye contact. I know they're going to succeed. I think at least half of them will go to university and get good jobs."

He knows there will be heartbreak, too.

"Some may leave and we may never see them anymore. That would really frickin' hurt but it happens," he said.

But, said Wayne, "This will always be family. We've got these kids in our will. They will always be part of our lives."

SINGING PRAISES OF FARMER SAUSAGE
December 31, 2007

ALTONA — All things have an end, goes an old German proverb.

Except wurst. It has two ends. Badabing!

But there seems no end to the farmer sausage and farmer sausage makers in Manitoba.

Manitoba is the centre of the universe for this Mennonite specialty. A recent foray into the Pembina Valley found no fewer than six different brands of farmer sausage on grocery shelves. There are at least another half dozen brands in Winnipeg and the rest of southern Manitoba.

Yet farmer sausage remains little more than a specialty food outside Mennonite circles.

"I love the stuff!" says Miriam Toews, whose award-winning novel, *A Complicated Kindness*, satirized life in a southern Manitoba Mennonite town.

But Toews doesn't know why farmer sausage hasn't come out of the closet into the mainstream diet either.

"I've always wondered why kolbasa gets all the love and our humble little Mennonite meat gets bupkas," she said in an e-mail exchange. "Maybe

Pioneer Meats president Scott Penner and farmer sausage

it's the name... Farmer sausage. Not sexy!! ... Farmer sausage sounds like maybe it's made out of farmers."

Pioneer Meats, just outside Altona, has been making virtually nothing but farmer sausage for 40 years. It produces about 455,000 kilograms a year for sale within Manitoba.

"It's us low-key Mennonites," Scott Penner, president of Pioneer Meats, said of farmer sausage's relative anonymity. "We wait for someone else to sex it up."

Well, how would you 'sex it up'? It's as straight-forward a food as there is. It's ground pork with a little salt and a little pepper, and smoked. That's very Mennonite. Going back in the religion's history, strong spices were forbidden.

Farmer sausage is lean. Pioneer's brand contains just 17 per cent fat. Neither is there filler like flour or wheat crumbs that you find in many sausages.

To prepare, you either fry it or boil it. For the latter, perforate a farmer sausage ring with a fork, boil it for three to four minutes, then let stand in the water for another six minutes. Little blobs of fat leak out the fork holes like a running nose. Scrape that off.

Tourists have been known to pick up old suitcases from a thrift store and stuff them full of Manitoba-made farmer sausage like it was contraband, before returning home, said Penner.

"We have people who come by and load up anywhere from 250 to 1,000 kilos of farmer sausage," he said. Someone from Leamington, Ontario, picked up 900 kilos.

There are many requests.

"Every week we get requests from places like Utah, Washington D.C., British Columbia, Nova Scotia," he said. "Someone called from Chicago who has a friend with restaurants and they wanted to put it on the menu."

But Pioneer Meats has only provincial status, so it can't sell outside Manitoba's borders. To become federally inspected, it would have to build a larger building, which is a possibility in the future, Penner said.

Eleanor Chornoboy, who has written books *Faspa — A Snack of*

Mennonite Stories, and *Snow Angels*, has converted some people to farmer sausage, too. "I have a girlfriend who lives outside San Diego and if I don't bring her farmer sausage when I visit, she gets very angry," she said.

Farmer sausage only really started to hit the Winnipeg supermarket chains in the 1980s. Penner Foods, the independent chain founded by the late Jim Penner that was eventually bought up by Sobey's, put Pioneer Meats "on the map," said Pioneer founder Bernie Penner, Scott's father.

After the Penner store on Henderson Highway stocked farmer sausage in 1981, other supermarket chains followed within two to four years, said Bernie.

Farmer sausage has spread beyond the Mennonite community, said Scott Penner. "It's a good seller in Gimli and there aren't too many Mennonites up there. It sells in Thompson, Flin Flon, Lynn Lake."

Even Mennonite communities like the Niagara Peninsula in Ontario don't seem to have a local farmer sausage maker. Saskatchewan and Alberta have some local brands, and there are brands made out of Abbotsford, B.C., and in some Mennonite communities in the United States.

But it's nothing compared to Manitoba.

Pioneer Meats, with 13 staff, makes a variety of farmer sausages including double smoked, with 33 per cent less salt, or a pork and beef mix. It also makes farmer sausage into hamburger patties and hotdogs for barbecuing.

ARTIST OF THE AGE OF RAIL
November 27, 2006

BRANDON — There's a little Rembrandt in paintings by Bill Hobbs and spectators always look for it.

Rembrandt is the nickname of the little Jack Russell terrier that often appears in Hobbs's art. It's a nod to the master Rembrandt who placed a similar dog, darkly lit, in his most famous painting, *The Night Watch*.

But in Hobbs's case, the dog doesn't scurry around musketeers in

Brandon artist Bill Hobbs

plumed hats and sashed waists. The dog is poised and possibly barking at old steam engine trains and train stations.

Some say Hobbs, a British-trained medical doctor and surgeon, now retired, is a master artist himself, although not well-known outside the rural Prairies. Critics note his excruciating precision. His paintings also preserve Canadian history.

"Once Bill is gone, his paintings are going to be like those of the Group of Seven," maintains Winnipeg art collector and dealer John Sogi, who also deals some of Hobbs's paintings. "Right now his paintings are going for $2,000 to $3,000 in Canada, but his daughter is selling a lot of his paintings in the United States for $10,000 to $15,000."

Hobbs's paintings touch a deep chord in the Prairie psyche, said Jennifer Woodbury, curator of the Art Gallery of Southwestern Manitoba in Brandon. Hobbs donates prints every year to help the gallery with fundraising and the public snaps them up.

That is, Prairie folk may have cursed the CNR and CPR for over a century but it's love, not hate, they feel for the old railway icons that Hobbs depicts. One can almost smell the smoke and grease coming off his great beastly steam engines, and his trains stations are from an era when they looked more like pavillions, many designed by famous Winnipeg architect Ralph Benjamin Pratt (1878–1950).

"People love train here," said Woodbury. She learned that after she moved to Brandon from Winnipeg. "Trains are very much a part of Manitoba, so much so that people build big expensive houses right next to railway tracks and no one seems to mind."

Hobbs, now 79, may not be a household name in urban centres but he's had his moments. One came in the early 1980s as the Bronfman family was celebrating an anniversary, likely the 75th, of Seagrams in Regina, where the family's booze empire began. The company held a cross-Canada art contest and the entries filled the posh Assiniboia Club. But Edgar Bronfman Sr. couldn't find a single painting to his liking. Finally, he looked up on the wall and spotted a Hobbs painting (a school bus in small town Esterhazy) that Hobbs had loaned to the club but was not entered in the contest. Who was that artist? Bronfman wanted to know. Why, that was just a painting by Dr. Hobbs whose medical office was down the street, someone said. (Hobbs originally immigrated to Saskatchewan.)

Bronfman shot out of the Assiniboia Club and strode down the street with half a dozen staffers in pursuit. The entourage crowded into Dr. Hobbs's little reception area behind Bronfman, who demanded to see the doctor. Bronfman gave Hobbs first prize and $25,000 for the rights to the print. Seagrams distributed a print of the painting with every purchase of a bottle of Seagrams whisky during the anniversary celebration.

Another Hobbs painting is the famous *40 Below Zero*, which shows cars parked diagonally outside the local cafe in Gainsborough, Saskatchewan. It beat out over 2,000 other entries to win a national contest in 1978.

More recently, Internet pharmacist Daren Jorgenson of Winnipeg bought 10 Hobbs originals, and five were purchased by Lorne Isfeld, who owns Autowest car dealership on McPhillips Street and Gimli Motors in Gimli.

But it's not all about the money for Hobbs. Locally, he has sold paintings to heritage groups at prices ranging from $800 to $1,500, "whatever they could afford," he said. Those sales included the rights to the prints so heritage groups could sell them to raise funds.

In fact, so many of his train stations are on display in rural town offices and museums that you could do a driving tour of them — if Hobbs could remember where they all are. Carberry and Neepawa town offices each have one, Hartney town office has two, and if you feel like a coffee then stop at Country Corner Cafe in Ninga to see another painting. A Hobbs painting also hangs in the Westoba Credit Union in Rivers, the Dauphin Rail Museum and the Beckoning Hills Museum in Boissevain.

The artist's love of trains goes back to his childhood in England. He became a keen model railroader as an adult. On his arrival in Canada in 1959, he even delivered a baby aboard the CPR passenger train that carried him to his first posting in Saskatchewan.

Hobbs was born in 1927 in Alderney in the Channel Islands. He was at the top of his class scholasticaly all through school, a level of scholarship that ran in the family. His brother, John Hobbs, was once nominated for a Nobel Prize for performing a new method of bone marrow transplant in the late 1990s. John later joined the Nobel judging committee.

Hobbs, the painter, studied fine art for four years at West of England Academy of Art but then came a bizarre career switch. Two weeks into the school year a student at Bristol University medical school was expelled for using heroin. The school knew Hobbs because he frequently visited to draw corpses for the medical students. They also knew he had the intelligence to be a physician. School officials began pushing Hobbs to fill the vacancy and he eventually consented.

He settled in Canada in 1959 as part of the great "brain drain" of medical graduates leaving England due to their unhappiness with socialized medicine. He set up practise as a physician and surgeon in Saskatchewan near the Manitoba border, and slowly began returning to his first love, painting. He moved to Ninga, south of Brandon which happened to be the home town of his second wife, Lois Washington, in the early 1990s, and to Brandon in 2002.

He displayed his Britishness during my visit by the paisley ascot he wore around his neck. "They're sensible wearing. They keep the chest warm," he said.

Besides Rembrandt, another of Hobbs's stock characters is a First Nation man wrapped in a Hudson Bay blanket standing on the railway platform. That was not an uncommon site on the Prairies, his research informed him.

"I have a tremendous love of railways. It keeps me going. And I'm especially into the time period. I can feel the atmosphere of what it must have been like in the 1920s and 30s."

BEAVER-SLAYER SAVES TACHE FROM MENACE
November 16, 2009

NEAR LORETTE — Beavers were having their way in the Rural Municipality of Tache on Winnipeg's eastern border, damming ditches, water diversions and even the Seine River.

Naomi Plett and a beaver pelt

Then came 13-year-old trapper Naomi Plett to the rescue. With her fur cap, uncertain smile and pigtails as thick as marine ropes, she looks like a female version of Davy Crockett.

Actually, Naomi was 12 when she first started trapping beavers. She trapped 15 beavers that first year. Since trapping season started October 1, she has already snared another 14. Some of them weigh up to 27 kilograms (60 lb).

"She's doing a really nice service for the municipality," Tache Councillor Bob Koop said.

You think of trappers as living in a log cabin deep in a forest with a wood stove for heat and snowshoes hung on a spike in the wall. But there is an abundance of wildlife right on Winnipeg's boundary.

"There's been so much water and rain the past couple years that the beavers are really spreading around," Councillor David Menard said.

The beavers dam up waterways that carry runoff into the Red River, causing water to back up and flood people's properties, he said.

Similar problems are occurring across the province. The North Interlake is having horrendous problems with beavers after all its rainfall and flooding the past couple of years. Some Manitoba municipalities have hired full-time animal-control officers to trap beavers, said Jack Dubois, provincial director of wildlife protection.

In Tache, beaver dams are being reported as large as 2.7 metres high that the municipality must get around to destroying with a backhoe.

"You have to get rid of the beaver first, otherwise they'll rebuild it. They'll rebuild the dam overnight. That's why they say 'eager like a beaver,'" Menard said.

The municipality has upped its bounty to $50 per head for problem beavers. That includes the $15 per head the province provides in its Problem Beaver Management Program. Trappers removed 7,600 beavers under the provincial program last year.

Naomi's dad, Darnell Plett, a pastor at Prairie Grove Fellowship Chapel here, said his daughter approached him a year ago about trapping beavers to help the community. A woman at church had complained that over half her stand of about 100 trees had been gnawed down by beavers.

Plett has another theory why his daughter decided she wanted to be a trapper.

"I think she wanted to forge an identity," he said. Naomi is the youngest child in an outdoorsy family that includes seven dogs, two horses, two cats, a dirt-bike riding brother, and 110 acres of prairie and bush next to the Seine River.

"She likes pioneer stuff, and making swords and throwing knives, and she did some bow-hunting for deer this fall," her dad said. Naomi's also into fishing and wilderness camping.

What does she enjoy about trapping? "The main part is spending time with my dad," she said. "And getting a little money."

The biggest challenge, Naomi said, is skinning the pelts. It takes her about two hours. She skins them, stretches and dries them, and then sells the pelts at a fur auction. Last year, she made about $20 a pelt, a terrible price and indicative of the poor market. A good price is double that.

She also saves the musk glands used in making perfume, which fetch another one or two dollars each.

All Naomi's trapping is within about three or four kilometres of the floodway, near Lorette. She has also started trapping foxes, raccoons and mink, and has even caught a coyote that was killing cattle on a farm.

Naomi gets a mixed reaction from kids her age, but her friends support her and are considering helping with skinning.

Dad allows he's had some awkward moments with parishioners who don't agree with the trapping. "We don't want to offend people," he said.

FROM CAMELS TO CATTLE
February 11, 2007

HODGSON — It's multiculturalism at its richest — and most improbable.

Muslim school kids here would teach curious classmates about their religion — and, kids being kids, their Arabic swear words.

They swapped school lunches, pita wraps for sliced bread, and even shared Ramadan, the month-long Muslim observance of dawn-to-dusk fasting. Some non-Muslim girls thought it might be a good way to diet.

"My friends used to fast with me," said Anne-Marie Omer, now an entry-level student at the University of Manitoba. "It made me feel really good that my friends would do that for me."

Long before there was a TV show called *Little Mosque on the Prairie* about a fictitious Muslim community on the Saskatchewan plains, Manitoba had its own Muslim community in Manitoba's Interlake, 165 kilometres north of Winnipeg. It still does.

"From camels to cattle," joked Joe Omer, Anne-Marie's father and one of five Muslim cattle ranchers still in this region just south of Peguis First Nation.

Cattle farmer Joe Omer and daughter Helen near Hodgson

And from olive groves to wheat fields.

Three Muslim families arrived from Lebanon in 1913-14 and scratched out a living by farming in the swampy, scruffy backwoods of the Interlake.

In fact, one of the three families, Alec and Jenny Abas, tried to come over on the *Titanic* in 1912 but were refused passage because it was full. They came over on Cunard Steamship Lines instead, but had friends who perished on the *Titanic*.

They arrived seeking opportunity.

Lebanese people have a reputation for being good at business and there are many examples here. Hilda Abas ran popular Hilda's Bakery and Restaurant in Hodgson for a dozen years. Earl Abas runs a health-food store and pawn shop in Fisher Branch, as well as his cattle ranch. Murvin Abas has owned and operated the pharmacy at the Percy Moore Hospital in Hodgson for the past 17 years. Ernest Abas was a local councillor for 30 years before stepping down recently. As the local marriage commissioner, he helped more than 100 couples tie the knot.

* * *

Hilda Abas would get up at three in the morning and bake 23 kilograms (50 lb) of flour into pita bread on an old wood stove. Her 12 children would awake to the aroma and taste of fresh bread.

Neighbours would drop in from miles around — you didn't phone first back then — for coffee and pita. Sometimes they'd be served those rich Lebanese pastries that drip with syrup. Or else they were introduced to falafel, hummus, or maybe what Muslim kids call "wheat burgers": ground beef and durum wheat mixed into a patty.

The Interlake Muslims were asked if they'd ever been looked down upon because they were different. Six interviews produced a single answer.

Never.

Since this is the Interlake, that's probably true. There is no dominant ethnic group. The Interlake is a gallimaufry of Scots, English, Icelanders, Ojibway, Métis, Ukrainians, Germans, Poles and others.

And helping one another is less duty in the Interlake than reflex, on the often execrably poor farmland. The Lebanese families originally settled in Crookston, Minnesota, but moved to the Interlake within a year, lured by Canada's Dominion Lands Act.

Two and three generations later, they can still remember the names of families who helped their ancestors. Ernest Abas, now 80, rattles off names like John Ross, Peter Sinclair and Billy Taylor.

"My parents [Alec and Jenny Abas] landed in Arborg by train in 1914. John Ross brought them here by a team of horses. The next day my father went to see the new land and it was just bush and swamp. Billy Taylor built my parents a temporary shack in two or three days for shelter."

Ghaly Abas, who moved to the Interlake from Lebanon to marry husband Boyd in 1980, found the same helping spirit.

Holly, as everyone calls her because it sounds closest to Ghaly, couldn't even speak English at first. She felt isolated on the farm. But neighbours helped. "A Mrs. Marie Finch visited me every day. She would put the money on the table and she'd say, 'This is 25 cents. This is 10 cents...'"

Today, cattle ranchers Boyd and Ghaly Abas have six children: the two youngest are at home, three are in university, and the oldest recently obtained his business degree and works in finance in Steinbach.

The Lebanese families observe religious rituals to varying degrees. Strict Muslim women dress in flowing raiments so only their hands, feet and faces show, when out in public. Women in the Interlake never went further than wearing a traditional head covering, called a *hijab*, and many do not. The dress is a woman's choice.

Strict Muslims will pray five times a day. It's not known how closely that timetable is followed here. "I miss [prayers]," one person said.

"The only food we don't eat is pork," explained Joe Omer. "Our Qur'an says don't eat the flesh of swine. Our neighbours respect that. If our kids are invited to a birthday party and they're serving hot dogs, the parents will tell us not to worry because they're having all-beef wieners."

Alcohol is also forbidden, "but we supplement that with plenty of coffee," said Omer.

Then there's Ramadan, where Muslims fast from dawn to dusk for a month. Everyone gets up at about 5:30 a.m. for breakfast, including the teenagers. Their next meal, and next coffee, isn't until nightfall.

"The first couple of days are hard but after that you get used to it," said Omer. You don't usually lose weight because you end up eating a big meal before going to bed, he said. Ramadan ends with a three-day celebration called Eid, which includes feasts and gifts.

Muslims recognize Jesus Christ as a sinless prophet but not the Son of God, and celebrate Christmas with just a family dinner.

There is no mosque here. The community never felt it was large enough to warrant one, and families still travel to Winnipeg for religious services.

There is a half-hour prayer service every Friday after lunch, however, in the nurse's residence at Percy Moore Hospital in Hodgson. These are led by the three Libyan doctors who started practising at the hospital two years ago. They are there because of the government's initiative to get more foreign-trained doctors practising in Manitoba.

Nine Muslim households remain in the Hodgson area, totalling about 40 people. Others have had to move to Winnipeg for economic opportunities.

As one of the more recent arrivals, Ghaly can verify that the differences between Lebanon and Manitoba are great. Summers are so short, she complains.

But mosquitoes aren't such a big issue. They have mosquitoes in Lebanon, too — smaller ones, but they bite harder, she said.

What bothers her are "bulldogs," as horseflies are called up here.

Ghaly has also learned about hockey. "I was scared the first [hockey game]. There were about 15 in the living room watching on TV, and when the team they were cheering for scored, they were jumping and throwing the cushions."

* * *

Like so many Lebanese people across Canada, many Muslims from the Interlake travelled to Lebanon last summer for vacation.

Shortly after they arrived, the bombs started to fall.

Israel began bombing Lebanon as reprisal for the kidnapping of three border guards by Lebanon extremist group Hezbollah. Estimates of infrastructure damages in Lebanon — including roads, bridges, power plants, sewer and water systems — start at $10 billion.

Both Israel and Lebanon are relatively small nations. Lebanon, at about 10,000 square kilometres, is about half the area of Israel.

Joe Omer's 13-year-old daughter Diane was visiting Lebanon at the time. His blood boils when he thinks of bombs dropping near his daughter. She managed to escape by crossing the border into Syria with a relative. Watching events on television, she saw the border crossing she had just used hours earlier get blown up. They returned safely under Canada's rescue program.

"It was scary, man," says her father.

Boyd Abas's mother Hilda was in Lebanon during the bombing, as were his sisters and sisters-in-law. Boyd and Ghaly were overwhelmed by the support from Interlake people.

"All of the Canadian people around here were so concerned because they knew Boyd's mother was there. Our phone never stopped ringing," said Ghaly. Added Boyd: "People were in tears even."

People have wondered why there were so many Canadians in Lebanon at the time.

"It's just like snowbirds," one community member explained. Lebanese Canadians routinely go to Lebanon — "the jewel of the Mediterranean" — for summer holidays.

Interlake Muslims are originally from the town of Kherbet Rouha in central Lebanon. It's interesting that large Lebanese communities in Edmonton, Calgary and London, Ontario, are also from the same small town. Many meet their future spouses while visiting Kherbet Rouha. Boyd Abas and his three brothers all met their future wives there and brought them back to Manitoba.

Kherbet Rouha is where Canada's Lebanese community congregated last summer.

"We Lebanese people, if you move here and don't go back to visit that town, you've sold out," said Murvin Abas, who runs the Fisher Pharmacy in Hodgson.

Murvin Abas, his wife, and four children were also in Kherbet Rouha last summer. It was his third time returning to Lebanon.

"Have you ever felt bombs hit the ground?" he asked. "It's the most humiliating feeling. A human being is actually dropping bombs on you." He is grateful the Canadian government rescued them.

Omer said neither Muslims nor Jews are responsible for policies in the Middle East.

"If he's here, he's a Canadian. I'm a Canadian," he said. "Lots of Jews here don't agree with the government there, just like people here don't like what Harper's doing."

Murvin has Jewish friends, including a friend of 15 years, Max Levitt. Their friendship is complicated by their strong attachment to their homelands.

Levitt, an independent financial counsellor, has children living in Israel and is a firm supporter of Israel.

How do they keep up their friendship?

"We've learned to understand one another," Murvin said. "I know the war's not between us. It's not between Arabs and Jews. It's always innocent people who die."

Said Levitt: "We have our discussions and sometimes we have words. His people think my people in Israel are to blame, and vice versa."

But, said Levitt, "we have to look beyond that... We have empathy for Lebanese people, and they have empathy for Israeli people."

* * *

Muslims, like most immigrants, typically settle in urban centres. For that reason, University of Manitoba students have trouble believing Anne-Marie Omer, an entry level university student, when she tells them she's from Hodgson. "They look at me like I'm crazy. They say, 'What are you doing up there?'"

(Lebanese settlers in rural Manitoba are not without precedent. Old-timers will recall the Forzley brothers originally settled in Sidney, east of

Brandon, before moving to Winnipeg and opening Boston Hat Works — a haberdashery that also fronted Manitoba's biggest illegal bookie operation in the 1950s.)

Annie-Marie praised the CBC's new comedy *Little Mosque on the Prairie*. "I think it's hilarious. I think it's totally a replica of what goes on, how men and women are always fighting, the rivalry between the men and the women."

Other people here have mixed feelings about the show but generally appreciate that it puts a human face on Muslims. Most people here complained the news media makes Muslims look like terrorists. Some people refused to be interviewed for that reason.

Anne-Marie is very proud of being Muslim and of her Interlake roots. "We bring a different flavour to the community," she said.

Fisher Branch farmer Paul Gregory agrees. The Muslims are funny and sociable, and "all entrepreneurs," said Gregory, whose kids play hockey with some of the boys.

"They're really well-liked in the community," said Gregory. "The plurality of our society is important. When you go to the States, it's a melting pot. Up here, our ethnicity is celebrated."

A CENTURY OF PAPER AND INK
December 22, 2007

ALTONA — There are a lot of great stories about book printer Friesens Corp., which celebrated its 100th anniversary this year (2007).

There's the story about how it became Canada's largest hardcover book printer, from such an unlikely location thousands of kilometres from its markets.

There's the story of how it reinvests $7 million a year in equipment, a colossal amount in the printing industry, to make itself the most modern

David Glenn Friesen (left) with
Curwin Friesen of Friesns Corp.

book- printing plant in the world.

And there's the story about how it employs 565 people in a town of just 3,400.

But the best story may be the one you hear only if you hang around Altona for awhile. It's about the lonely union reps who are sometimes assigned to recruit at Friesens.

A union organizer from Winnipeg will visit every few years to sell employees on the idea of unionizing. Employees will listen politely (because they're small-town folk and are hospitable to visitors), say they'll think about it, escort the union rep back to his or her car, then forget everything they just heard.

Why would they unionize? Journeymen, like pressmen, earn more than $50,000 after five years. That's 10 to 15 per cent higher than any other employees in southern Manitoba, according to a Pembina Valley Development Corp. survey. It's also higher than any competitor in the United States.

And that's before the extras. Friesens has a profit-sharing plan. It's based on how the company performs, of course. But the profit-sharing has been paying out on average about five weeks' extra salary per employee. That works out to a 10 per cent bonus.

It gets better. The employees also own the company. Repeat: The

ALTONA OPENS GALLERY IN THE PARK
JULY 26, 2008

ALTONA — It's the first bona fide tourist attraction to open in southern Manitoba in years and visitors are forewarned: bring along your superlatives.

Altona and Friesens Corporation unveiled its Gallery in the Park in the summer of 2008, an art house and sculpture garden that is of a quality you'd expect when Friesens puts its name behind something.

This is not a small town erecting a giant roadside monument of an animal or bug. This is a marvelous array of local and North American art.

The Schwartz House, a refurbished three-storey clapboard heritage home built in 1902, houses paintings and small sculptures. The featured artist occupies the main floor, while works by local artists are upstairs.

Up to 50 outdoor statues beautify the outdoor grounds designed by Gary Hilderman of Hilderman Thomas Frank Cram Landscape

Peter Sawatzky and his caribou sculpture in the Schmidt House

employees own the company.

A share program was implemented in the early 1980s. Only employees can own shares, so there are no outside shareholders or mutual fund managers dictating how the company is run.

Architecture of Winnipeg. The garden sightlines are amazing. The garden includes two ponds connected by a channel, and a six-metre (20 ft) fountain at the opposite end from the Schwartz House.

"We really believe this will get art people to drive out from Winnipeg," Curwin Friesen, president and CEO of Friesens said.

Friesens spearheaded the $1.2-million project, footing nearly half the cost but company officials stressed it is a community project. Other local businesses contributed $300,000, and there was also private fundraising. The Richardson Foundation and Thomas Sill Foundation each donated $100,000.

Famed Manitoba sculptor Peter Sawatzky was the gallery's featured artist the first year. In 2011, featured artists were Bill Pura of Winnipeg for the first part of the year, and Shirley Elias and Bette Woodlands for the second half of the year.

Sawatzky said people may be surprised to find a sculpture garden in a small town like Altona that is equal to the Leo Mol Sculpture Garden in Assiniboine Park. (There is a Leo Mol sculpture in the Altona gardens, too.)

"[Gallery in the Park] has a different atmosphere. It's much more open where you can see a lot of the garden from different perspectives. The Leo Mol garden has a lot of quiet spaces," Sawatzky said.

The gallery tries to buy a major new art piece every year. In 2011, it purchased a bronze statue entitled "The Gossips" by Rose-Aimée Bélanger for $65,000.

The gallery and gardens open about the third week in May. The gallery closes at the end of September. The gardens stay open a month longer. See galleryinthepark.com for more details.

The shares pay out annual dividends. Those dividends have been averaging an extra $3.5 million a year in recent times to the over 500 employees who have bought shares (they're not given away). Payments depend on a person's holdings, but they average more than $5,000 each.

Finally, there's the appreciation on those shares. Share value is based on audited book value of the company, not on public trading like a listed company. As of October 31, 2007 the share price was $6.79. That may not sound like much, but the shares started out as penny stock and have split five or six times.

What it means is that some shareholder employees have done well — very well. Some employees have become millionaires from their shares alone.

Since 1999, at least nine employees and likely more have cashed out shares upon retirement — only employees can own shares, remember — worth more than $1 million each. And these aren't just top-ranked executives but include guys on the floor, like paper cutters, who have been with the company a long time and who reinvested their dividends into shares. For other employees, the share program has allowed them to retire in their mid-50s. (Employees also have a pension plan and full Blue Cross coverage.)

"The people who have 'em, love 'em," said a man in the Altona Motor Hotel beverage room, referring to the shares. (Unlike some Mennonite towns, Altona not only has a beverage room and beer vendor, but wet lounges and a liquor commission outlet, and has had them for as long as anyone can remember.)

How does Friesens do it? Employee ownership, says David Glenn Friesen, the third-generation Friesen to run the company since founder David W. Friesen, and the company president who masterfully guided the company the last three decades before retiring this summer.

"We have a fabulous staff who are working their hearts out for themselves... as opposed to for some rich guy," said David Glenn. "So they're not booking off sick on Monday. They're not booking off sick on Friday. They're not putting sand in the gears. They're building a future for themselves and their families."

Wow.

People say wow a lot when they visit Friesens. The first time Great Plains Publishing president Gregg Shilliday visited 15 years ago for his *Manitoba 125,* a three-volume history of Manitoba, he couldn't find Friesens. He went past some buildings he assumed was the hospital and finally stopped at a gas station to ask for directions. Of course, the complex he thought was a hospital was Friesens.

Wow is what people say when they see the flawless, high-end books Friesens produces.

And wow is what people say when they step into its printing plant. The plant looks more like something out of a Stanley Kubrick science fiction movie. It's almost all white — a matte white without any glare — and spotless.

White? Spotless? Remember, this is a printing plant and printing plants the world over are dark, dingy places with dust and ink smears everywhere and more litter on the floor than after the Shrine Circus.

"At the end of each year, we paint the walls, all the [ceiling] pipes are vacuumed, the floors are resurfaced, because it's the employees' equipment," said Curwin Friesen, the company's youthful new president.

Everything in the plant is new, too. There are six lanes of conveyor belts, each about 40 metres long, all with some component of book assemblage careering down their rubber treadmills. There are computer screens for new paperless proofing. There is a "perfect binder" purchased from Germany two years ago that lays glue down the book spine.

Then there's a large robot bought in Japan, which looks like it's right out of the old *Lost in Space* television show, that stacks boxes of books onto pallets. "It's to reduce repetitive-motion stress," explained Curwin Friesen.

Why does Friesens Corp. own $50 million of the best printing equipment in the world? Because it has to. Because if you're going to be located in Altona, and you expect clients in Toronto to visit and do business with you, and expect clients in New York to visit and do business with you, and in Vancouver and overseas, etc., you better not be just another printing plant

"I'm a big believer in [Winnipeg entrepreneur and author] Sheldon Bowles's saying, 'You got to have raving fans,'" said David Glenn. "There isn't anyone who comes here who isn't impressed."

Then you combine that with small-town service. "Their customer service is exceptional," says Altona-based writer Les Kletke, who has self-published six books, all at Friesens. "Even though I only have 2,000 books printed, they treat you like you're their biggest customer. Even the guys on the loading dock come out to congratulate you."

You'd think the ongoing technological improvement would result in mass layoffs, but it hasn't. Staffing has been pretty consistent at 560 people in recent years. The company has simply continued to grow its market. Another 100 or so people work the sales offices across North America.

The David Glenn Friesen era saw him take the company from a couple hundred employees in the late 1970s, to 675 today. He has moved the plant from a single shift, to two shifts, to 24/6 production. The plant is closed on the Sabbath.

Implementing shifts was tough, and some people left the company over it, even extended family members. It's also tough on staff, but it's the only way to maximize the returns out of the equipment, especially with the rising Canadian dollar. (A surprising number of plants in southern Manitoba operate 24 hours, like Decor Cabinets in Morden, Triple E and Lode King in Winkler and Loewen Windows in Steinbach.)

David Glenn's biggest decision was narrowing the company's production mix. It was into printing newspapers, wholesale stationery and commercial printing, as well as books, when he took over.

"If the company was to succeed, we had to specialize and we had to be in product that travelled well, and books are probably one of the best," he said.

He also developed the company's yearbook division, which has its own

100,000 square-foot plant. And he found ways to overcome the obstacles of operating out of Altona, an hour's drive south of Winnipeg.

That is, if Friesens were based in Toronto, a delivery truck would simply pick up its finished books and drive them across town to McClelland & Stewart. If Friesens were in Winnipeg, a third-party carrier would pick up the books and send them by air to Toronto, where a delivery truck would deliver them to McClelland & Stewart.

But because Friesens is in Altona, the company had to buy its own fleet of trucks to deliver books to the airport. It's the only book printer in Canada that has a truck fleet. Ten trucks go back and forth to Winnipeg all day long. For years, Friesens couldn't even get couriers to drive out to Altona to transport proofs — a sample copy of the book layout before it goes to print.

Taxes are also higher in a small rural community because there is a smaller tax base to pay for services like water and sewers. Telephone costs are higher for obvious reasons. Friesens used to rent phone lines for $1,200 a month from Manitoba Telecom Services. And it's hard to find staff. That's one reason why wages are so solid.

However, Friesens also turns disadvantages into advantages. Because it is removed from a major urban centre, it can't farm out some processes like pre-press or binding like other printers. So it has to do the entire process itself.

"When something goes wrong, what was happening [with other printers] was the printer was blaming the colour house if a customer didn't like the colour, and the binder was blaming the printer, and the printer was blaming the binder," said David Glenn. "We could go to a customer and say, 'If there's a problem, you deal with us.'"

Its biggest advantage, however, is staff. Every company says that today, but it's really true here. The commitment from staff is not only for what's best for themselves and their families, but for what will sustain the company, and therefore the community. Friesens is the lifeline for Altona, which plays second fiddle to larger Mennonite communities like Winkler and Steinbach.

"This company was built originally to provide employment in town," said David Glenn. "When my father and his brothers were finished, they didn't say, 'Let's take the money and split it up and let everyone else start over.' Their goal was to have a healthy community.

"Whatever money the company has made has always gone back into the company. It hasn't gone to an owner and managers and heaven knows what else."

Friesens supports the community in countless ways. For its 100th anniversary, it threw a giant party attended by more than 1,000 people, with a free concert and food. It also handed out a new coffee-table book on Altona, and a hardcover children's book, *A Is For Altona*. It co-published the *Encyclopedia of Manitoba* with Great Plains Publications. And something people will be hearing a lot more about soon is its new $1 million art gallery and sculpture waterpark that seems almost guaranteed to be a new Manitoba tourist destination.

It's building a new black-and-white book plant, to go with its 125,000 and 100,000 square-foot plants for colour book printing and yearbook printing.

It's also headed into uncharted waters. Although his surname is Friesen, Curwin Friesen is the first president not from the bloodline of its founder. David Glenn Friesen is chairman of the board.

The timing hasn't been great for Curwin. The Canadian dollar has risen 20 per cent against the U.S. dollar in the last year, which will make past dividends and profit shares for employees difficult to maintain. Friesens has ramped up production by 10 to 15 per cent to make up for reduced margins, by going from 24/5 shifts to 24/6.

Curwin, 37, is a native of Altona who studied economics at the University of Waterloo, earning the Governor General's Award for highest academic average. He has also taken courses at Harvard and worked on Bay Street before returning to his hometown.

"We've been in business 100 years. We are celebrating that, but we're more interested in the next year. Longevity doesn't mean we'll be around forever," he said.

Just don't send any doomsday talk his way about how e-books are going to kill print.

"E-books most likely will have a niche in the future. But I'll remind you that when radio first came out, books were going to be dead. And when TV first came out, radio and books were going to be dead. [But] communication tends to grow, not shrink," he said.

"The Internet is a boon to us in some ways. Publishers can publish all kinds of esoteric work that they couldn't publish before because they can actually find customers via the Internet." New technologies are also making printing books cheaper and are allowing printers to make shorter runs, he said.

THE BOOK ON FRIESENS CORP.

A snapshot of Friesens Corp., Canada's largest hardcover book printer:

- Friesens prints 25 million books a year on 4,000 to 6,000 book titles.
- About 40 percent of its business was in the United States the past year.
- Friesens Corp. employs 640 people. About 565 are in Altona and the rest are in sales offices across North America.
- Friesens has sales offices across Canada, including Toronto, Montreal and Vancouver. Its offices in the United States include Boston, Denver, Chicago, New York, Oklahoma City, Minneapolis and San Francisco.
- It has printed 25 million copies of the Robert Munsch children's book, *Love You Forever*.
- Ten percent of the company's profit before taxes is returned to employees each year in a profit-sharing agreement.
- Freisens has been awarded the status of one of Canada's 50 best-managed companies for nearly a decade.

MINNEDOSA MAN BANISHES THE DARK
April 6, 2003

This was written during the early days of George W. Bush's foray into Iraq in search of weapons of mass destruction. Canadian Photonics is still operating out of Minnedosa.

MINNEDOSA — There's been great controversy over who supplied Iraq with night-vision goggles — Russia? Syria? — in its war against the American-led coalition.

But there's been no mention at all about where American troops in Iraq, and NATO forces in Afghanistan, obtained their night-vision goggles and cameras.

Mark Wahoski holds a micro camera

Would you believe Minnedosa?

A small high-tech firm based here along the Yellowhead Highway is the designer and manufacturer of night-vision equipment used by NATO forces in Afghanistan. The United States military also is a major buyer of night-vision goggles from Canadian Photonics Labs Inc., although the company cannot confirm if the equipment is being used in Iraq.

Canadian Photonics is the brainchild of Mark Wahoski, who was born and raised on a grain-and-livestock farm near this town of 2,400, about 200 kilometres west of Winnipeg.

"We're very proud to do our part to fight terrorism," said Wahoski. "What we all want is a safer world for our kids."

Wahoski is restricted in what he can say about sales of night-vision equipment because it is for military use. However, he can say at least 1,000 of the company's night-vision cameras and goggles are being used by NATO forces in the Persian Gulf right now. This is specialized equipment at the high end of that type of technology. But Wahoski refused to divulge how the equipment is specialized.

"At the end of the day, those products have to protect us. That's why the military is so secretive," he said.

The company is also scrupulous about whom it deals with. "We don't sell anything military outside NATO. We're very strict about that," said Wahoski, who occasionally uses the goggles himself to spot wildlife at night in the scenic valleys surrounding Minnedosa.

The price of night-vision equipment ranges from $70 to $45,000, depending on the quality.

Canadian Photonics is located in downtown Minnedosa, where it began eight years ago. It has just about the smallest storefront sign ever made. Its name is printed in small type on a letter-sized sheet of paper.

Half of Canadian Photonics' dozen employees are engineers. Wahoski, 41, scouted the globe to bring highly skilled engineers to this region. That has been one of the challenges of operating in a small, rural centre like Minnedosa. His stable of employees includes engineers from Ukraine, Singapore, Moscow and Shanghai, as well as Canadian-trained engineers. He also has salesman working on commission around the world.

Photonics is not a household word but it might be in the future. Photonics is the marriage of light energy and electronics — a photon is a particle of light. Wahoski saw unlimited opportunity in photonics a decade ago when the Internet started and triggered the need for digital imaging.

Satellite telephones used by news correspondents in the Persian Gulf are an example of photonics. An image captured through a lens is recorded digitally, then beamed to a satellite, which beams it back down to a fibre-optic cable, which carries the image to our television and computer screens.

Wahoski is guarded about the success of Canadian Photonics but allows it is doing well.

"With high-tech, you do get rewarded if your product is successful, and we have had successful products," Wahoski said. "We focus on niche markets, but niche markets can be pretty good if they've got legs."

Canadian Photonics is proof you can set up business anywhere in today's high-tech world. The company is not only away from a major urban centre, but also a long way from Canada's photonics centre in Ottawa, where the federal government recently dropped $30 million to cluster the industry into a photonics park in conjunction with Carleton University. Wahoski wasn't even aware of the federal subsidy.

Wahoski said he chooses to do business and raise a family here because it's where he's from and he prefers the rural lifestyle.

Canadian Photonics has rented a production line in Korea to assemble its products that has been running for the past three years. The company also operates an occasional production line in Taiwan. The cost of labour in those regions is lower and the quality of labour for electronics assembly is high, Wahoski explained.

"All major electronics producers have operations offshore," Wahoski said, maintaining his company must do the same to remain competitive.

Wahoski believes the goggles used by Iraqi troops are likely very low-end technology that allows users to only see vague body outlines. The night vision used by NATO forces allows soldiers to see as if it were daylight.

Another product Canadian Photonics is proud of is one of the world's fastest cameras. The camera shoots 400,000 frames per second. The frames then can be played back in slow motion.

NATO members use the company's high-speed cameras to do research, such as in designing a better bullet-proof vest.

The cameras also are used by various manufacturing companies to detect problems in their assembly lines. As production of everything from sausages to motor vehicles becomes faster and faster, the cameras are used to find problems. "It may be something as simple as a bent screw, but the camera can see it and alert the company," Wahoski said. "Automation has become faster and faster, and now we need faster tools to deal with it."

One Canadian Photonics client is a South African company that is designing special boots for people who work in land-mine detection. The high-speed camera records the blast from a land mine, so the boot manufacturer can study the pattern of energy from such an explosion. From that, it is trying to design a boot that can absorb the blast without injuring the wearer.

"It's very intriguing and very exciting work. You're helping to make a difference," said Wahoski.

Wahoski became involved in photonics a decade ago when a friend in Australia, who raised emus, approached him with a problem: How to detect whether an emu egg embryo was alive. The matter was crucial to sales of emu eggs, which are very expensive.

Wahoski developed an infrared camera that could see through the egg shell and tell whether the embryo had a heartbeat. Wahoski had no idea how much demand there would be for his invention. He went to various agricultural trade shows and sales took off globally. That served as the embryo, too, of his company.

Entrepreneurship runs in the Wahoski family. Mark is one of six brothers who all operate their own companies.

Wahoski's day starts at 7:30 a.m. and runs until 10 p.m. or midnight each night. It's the price of being in a global business. "At the start of our day, Europe's been up for six hours already, so I need to come in early," he explained. "At 6 p.m. our time, Asia and Australia are just coming to work."

In today's world, customers expect same-day service. "People have become accustomed to getting an answer right now. People send out an e-mail and they want an e-mail back almost instantly," he said.

Meanwhile, his three kids will stop by the office to have lunch with dad, and he still has supper every night with his family. His kids are equipped with two-way radios if they go anywhere of any distance, like to the nearby beach. "If I had a business somewhere else, it would mean either a lot less time for the business, or a lot less with my family," said Wahoski.

"We're having a helluva good time doing what we're doing."

CATALOGUE HOUSE ON THE PRAIRIE
January 8, 2007

SPERLING — In 1907, Harry "Yankee" Brown of Rockford, Illinois, bought the equivalent of swamp land in Florida, only it was in central Manitoba.

The land had been purchased by a realtor for $5,200 a year earlier. The realtor then flipped it to Brown, a Chicago-area farmer, for $25,800.

Those were the days. But they were also the days when you could order your house from an Eaton's catalogue.

Gordon and Mona Brown's Eaton house near Sperling

Brown drained the land, and, by 1917, could afford his dream home: Model No. 674 in the Eaton's *Modern Homes, Building and Material* catalogue.

That magnificent two-and-a-half-storey home still stands today, splendidly maintained by fourth-generation owners Gordon and Mona Brown.

"It's the grandest Eaton house in Western Canada. I don't think there's any question," said Les Henry, Saskatchewan author of *Catalogue Homes: Eaton's and Others*, in a telephone interview.

The Brown house, hidden away down a gravel farm road east of Carman, 45 kilometres west of Winnipeg, is worthy of being profiled in one of those glossy magazines of all the posh homes.

"It's just kind of stunning. It's a mansion," said Henry, who said he "can remember every minute" of his tour of the Brown home.

The home is also more proof that Eaton's, the former department store giant, thought of everything. The home came with a dumbwaiter (a pulley system for hauling preservatives from the basement to the kitchen), a clothes chute spanning three floors, an original 32-volt wind generator for electricity, and even a turn-of-the-century central vacuum system, if you can believe it. (It's been removed, but the vacuum and pipes are still stored in a shed.)

It has piano windows that make prisms inside the house when the sunlight hits a certain way, a rooftop widow's walk, and there was also once a second-storey verandah.

And much more. Eaton's even came up with a landscape design that included tennis courts for "Yankee" Brown — local people nicknamed him "Yankee" because he refused to take out Canadian citizenship — had a fetish for wearing bow ties and always threw huge Fourth of July barn dances.

Eaton's only sold its houses on the rural Prairies, and homes were only included in its Winnipeg catalogues. The rural Prairies was a fairly captive market because farmers had no nearby building supply centres. The Eaton homes were called kit homes because they were shipped direct from British Columbia in rail boxcars complete with everything: lumber, shingles, nails, doors, door knobs, light fixtures, etc. Farmers usually hired a contractor to

Gordon Brown in his living room

put up the house. The Browns have the blueprints for their home framed on the wall.

The year 1917 was the biggest year for Eaton home sales because post-First World War wheat prices hit a record high for the century: $28 a bushel, adjusted for inflation, said Henry. Today, $5 a bushel is considered a decent price.

Harry and Fannie Brown's home cost $8,000, about $120,000 in today's dollars. It has 12 rooms: parlour, den, dining room, pantry, summer kitchen (to keep the house from getting too hot), third-storey attic (one big recreation room with the original billiard table still in the centre), bathroom and five bedrooms.

What Eaton's didn't account for was central Manitoba's Osborne clay. It is even more problematic than the gumbo along the Red River in how it expands and contracts with moisture levels. "During the droughts of the 1960s, one night there was a big bang and the foundation on the north side of the house had buckled," Gordon Brown said during a tour.

Contractors had to dig up and repair the footings, and removed the second floor verandah in the process.

The original cedar shake shingles lasted 60 years. The main floor has fir hardwood floors, and the second floor hardwood is maple.

Gordon and Mona Brown bought the home in 1980 and converted it from coal heat to electrical radiated hot water heat. Gordon's father would go through 20 tonnes of coal a winter.

The walls are amazing. They include two inner walls of shiplap. Plywood wasn't invented yet so builders made walls of interlocking boards called shiplap. Air trapped between the foot-thick walls was supposed to help keep out the cold, but only minimally.

Insulation has since replaced air between the walls.

Harry and Fannie named their farm Lone Star Farm because they were also considering moving to Texas before deciding on Manitoba, and that is still its name today. Gordon Brown still farms about 1,100 acres.

(Several hundred relatives showed up when Gordon and Mona hosted the 100th anniversary of the Brown family settling in Manitoba in 2008.)

HOUSE IN A BOX
January 28, 2007

LAC DU BONNET — Anyone who could "swing a hammer" could build an Aladdin home, the company's catalogues advertised a century ago.

And many rural people did.

Like Eaton's catalogue homes, all the lumber and fixtures arrived by boxcar, shipped from mill yards in British Columbia,

But unlike Eaton's homes, the lumber for Aladdin homes was all pre-cut and numbered. Like a giant children's toy at Christmas, you just followed the numbers and put it together yourself.

"Each section had a letter, and then section boards were numbered. You put A1 to A1, and B2 to B2…" said Bert Towle, whose parents Victor and

Ella Towle built an Aladdin farm house near Beausejour in 1929.

In 1999, Anthony Kost and Shawn Tester purchased what remained of the abandoned, two-storey Towle home for $2,500, and spent $7,000 moving it to a wooded lot near Lac du Bonnet.

Today, the home is a Prairie-Shield treasure — located on the approximate dividing line between the Prairies and Canadian Shield, 90 kilometres east of Winnipeg.

The couple spent hundreds of thousands of dollars replacing the roof,

Aladdin house near Lac du Bonnet

stucco, plaster, and windows; refinishing all the hardwood floors and wood trim; and installing plumbing, electricity, and geothermal heating.

"We designed the remaking of the house on the computer, just the two of us," said Shawn.

They also added a 1,100 square-foot addition to the original 1,200-square-foot home, using materials from the second floor so you can't tell new from old.

The Aladdin home's eight-acre yard has been beautifully landscaped, including an acre-sized pond for swimming in summer, and skating in win-

Shawn Tester inside the living area of her Aladdin house

ter. The family tried stocking it with fish last year until an otter moved in.

The pond was originally a "borrow pit" where soil was dug to raise the home four feet above ground level. The basement then didn't have to be dug so deep, and it allows for more light in the basement.

The couple recently sold the home so they could be closer to Anthony's job as a computer programmer in Winnipeg. It was a very difficult move emotionally.

"The process of letting go of the house takes time, and it's still not easy," said Shawn. New owners agreed to let the *Free Press* tour the home.

The Aladdin home is so much sturdier than most homes in Winnipeg. Most of the wood is solid, old growth fir you can't buy anymore. The fir also hardens with time.

"The wood came from Douglas fir trees that were 200 feet to the first limb, so there were no knots," said Les Henry, author of *Catalogue Homes: Eaton's and Others*, in a telephone interview from Saskatoon. In fact, Aladdin offered $1 for every knot a customer found in a carload of Aladdin lumber.

Former department store giant Eaton's sold catalogue homes from 1910-

32, and stopped when the market dried up during the Great Depression. Sears sold catalogue homes from 1908–40 but only in the United States.

But American company Aladdin started in 1905 and sold catalogue homes in Canada until 1952, and into the 1980s in the U.S., said Henry. Many more Aladdin homes were built in Western Canada than Eaton's homes, since Aladdin was around longer, he said.

"If you go on eBay, you can buy a 1919 American Aladdin home," Henry said.

The Aladdin home in Lac du Bonnet originally had a wind-power generator feeding batteries in the basement, for limited electricity.

Anthony and Shawn restored the maple hardwood floors on the main floor, and fir floors upstairs. They added an outdoor hot tub, and three gas fireplaces, modified to run on propane.

There is even a hockey room in the basement. The concrete floors and wall have more black marks from pucks and sticks than a Gerry Cheevers goalie mask. In their Winnipeg home, the couple's 11-year-old son Lucas has already broken a wall lamp playing hockey where he wasn't supposed to — in his room. "Lucas misses [the hockey room] big time," said mom, Shawn.

HOUSE BURROWED INTO EARTH CHEAP TO HEAT
January 26, 2009

NEAR MACGREGOR — So what does it cost Cam and Lisa Cleaver to heat their home, nestled in a gorgeous 22-acre woodlot atop the Manitoba escarpment?

Twenty bucks.

No, but seriously, what do you pay to heat your home?

Twenty bucks — the same as they've paid every year for the past 14 years.

Oh well, they must live in a shack, you're thinking.

No. At 2,500 square feet, their house is probably bigger than yours.

The Cleavers live in one of only two known underground homes in Manitoba but theirs is all the more fantastic for its location — burrowed into the top of a hill.

Cam and Lisa Cleaver outside their underground home

In fact, it's located right on the line where the escarpment begins. Ten thousand years ago, it might have been a beach house on Lake Agassiz.

There are two reasons the Cleavers have virtually no heating cost. First, they are embedded in at least 1.5 metres (5 ft) of earth on all sides (except the south side, to maximize sunshine for light and warmth). At anything more than 1.2 metres (4 ft) below ground, temperatures are a steady 10° to 12° Celsius.

So the Cleaver home only has to be heated 8 to 10 degrees above the soil temperature to be made livable. That's compared to most houses which have to be heated against the outside air temperature. They need no air conditioning in summer because the earth cools their residence.

The second reason their heating cost is so low is they live in a forested area and use an outdoor boiler. Cam and the kids take the pickup truck each fall to gather and cut deadfall. The $20 is the gas for the truck and chainsaw.

They feed the boiler once a day and burn about four cords (a 4 x 4 x 8-foot stack) each year, but that's also to continuously heat a workshop separate from the house. Even if they paid for the four cords of firewood, it would only cost in the $400 range, depending on the type of wood.

On a day when it was worse than -40° Celsius with the wind chill, their home was unbelievably cosy inside, especially with its radiant floor heat.

Cam built the underground home 15 years ago, working evenings after his day job. He was frequently interrupted by gawkers who stopped by to shake their heads and tell him to expect a visit from some men in white suits. "Everyone thought I was a lunatic," Cam said.

Wife Lisa included? Well, let's just say she went from being a city girl from Winnipeg's North End to a country gal when she met Cam, to one of the mole people.

Cam originally bought the property as a place to hunt. He got his idea after visiting cousins in Wichita, Kansas, where he spotted a house piled with dirt to keep it cool in summer.

The floors, walls and ceiling of the Cleaver home are concrete. Cam knew concrete because he was employed at the time by a company that built concrete septic pools for large hog farms.

The home's inside walls have been textured so they look like a stylish stucco. The ceiling is a story in itself. Cam erected 500 two-by-four studs, one foot apart, to hold a plywood platform while concrete was poured over top. The studs were removed once the concrete hardened.

When you build with concrete, you have to plan in advance for things such as switches and electric plugs, because you can't make new holes later.

Cam almost forgot the dryer vent. Just as the concrete was being poured, he shouted for the operator to stop so he could make the adjustment.

The home is 30 metres (100 ft) long by 7.6 metres (25 ft) wide. "It's like a long trailer home," said Cam, although it's much wider. From the front, it looks like a one-storey school, or even a little strip mall, although that sounds uncharitable and the description isn't meant to be.

The bedrooms and main rooms, such as the den and living room, all face south to obtain natural light. The bathroom is on the other side and has no windows. Lisa said it's like living in an apartment and not an issue.

It's also the safest kind of building in a tornado. There were two tornados in the general area last summer, including one south of the town of Holland.

Their kids love the house, plus the giant playground of 22 acres of hilly woods around it.

Cam has a word of caution for anyone wanting to duplicate his feat though. Lenders will not grant a mortgage on an unconventional house, he said. He had to take a regular loan like you'd get for buying a car, at a higher interest rate.

Limestone cliffs at Steep Rock on Lake Manitoba.

The Lake

GANDOLFINI BUYS LOT ON LAKE MANITOBA
October 12, 2007

Chad Olafson is about to find out how Tony Soprano deals with stool pigeons.

Olafson is the young entrepreneur behind a hot new cottage development at Lake Manitoba Narrows, where he has sold almost 290 lots in just nine months.

But he recently let slip that one of his buyers is none other than mega-celebrity James Gandolfini, who played the role of mob boss Tony Soprano on the hit TV series *The Sopranos.*

Not only is Gandolfini one of today's biggest stars, famous for playing a gangster who hired hit men to take care of characters who crossed him, he is also one of the most private and publicity shy actors and rarely grants interviews.

"I don't know if he would be too happy if a lot of people knew," said Olafson, when approached with the news tip that Gandolfini bought a cottage lot from him.

James Gandolfini

Too late, Chad.

Other members of Gandolfini's family were actually first to discover this provincial gem where Lake Manitoba bottlenecks like an hourglass, 200 kilometres north of Winnipeg. Two other members of the actor's family bought their properties first.

Gandolfini's brother-in-law, Eddie, used to visit

Chad Olafson

Lake Manitoba Narrows Lodge, owned by Olafson's family, to hunt. He became good friends with Chad, 32. The brother-in-law and Gandolfini's sister, Joanna, even attended Olafson's wedding. "They both flew down from Manhattan," said Olafson.

This was before hit series *The Sopranos* began in 1999, starring New Jersey-born James Gandolfini.

"[Eddie] said to me that his brother-in-law was a struggling actor, so if you're ever in New York, maybe he can get you in to see something," said Olafson.

"[Gandolfini] had been in a couple of things by then but nothing famous. He was in the movie *True Romance*. Then he just got super famous super fast."

Olafson, who grew up on an Interlake cattle ranch his father, Blair, still runs, has visited the Gandolfini family in New York. "We went to see [Broadway musical] *The Producers* — James took us to that — and he said let's go for drinks after."

So they went to none other than famous New York landmark Sardi's Restaurant in Times Square. "It was funny. We walked out of Sardi's and right next to [Gandolfini] was this 24-metre (80 ft) poster of him in Times Square. I said to him 'that must make your head feel pretty big, eh man?'"

What did he say? "Aw, nothing. He jokes about how I say 'eh?' all the time."

The last time Olafson and his wife, Brandee, visited New York, he talked to Gandolfini beforehand by phone. "He said, 'Anything you want in New York, you just name it.'" Olafson didn't want to impose on his friend but mentioned it had always been a dream of his to see *Saturday Night Live*.

"He got us front-row tickets," said Olafson. They met Gandolfini later for dinner at a Manhattan restaurant the actor co-owns.

"He couldn't do anything with us afterward because he was busy, but he gave us his limo for the rest of the night. We just had his chauffeur drive us around Manhattan all night. It was great."

Gandolfini looked at properties in Montana before deciding to buy in Lake Manitoba Narrows. Olafson said Gandolfini hasn't fished or hunted there but likes snowmobiling, boating, riding around on ATVs, "and getting away. He's actually pretty quiet."

Olafson wondered if there was any way to suppress news of Gandolfini's interest in the area. He wasn't pleading with the *Free Press* but did sound worried. Gandolfini has managed to visit without fanfare in the past. "He likes coming out because not too many people know about the place. If people know about it too much..."

However, that kind of news is unlikely to stay secret for long.

Olafson's cottage development is also not well-known. He bought 720 acres — including a mile of shoreline on the west side of Lake Manitoba, south of the Narrows bridge — for $2.3 million last December. He immediately began clearing land and building roads.

The lots are not on Laurentian rock, or on sandy Lake Winnipeg shoreline, like many Manitoba cottages. The shoreline can be marshy and the lake is known more for fishing than other recreation.

But when Olafson put his lots up for sale on the market in Alberta, they took off.

"I went to the Home Expression Show in Edmonton," he said. "They sold like crazy. I sold 20 lots a day for a week, 150 lots in one week. It was just ridiculous.

"So many people from Alberta are originally from Manitoba. They move out to follow the oil money. Now they don't want to live there."

About 85 per cent of the 290 lots sold so far have gone to Albertans.

"In Alberta, it's $1 million to live on a lake and the lake is a slough, from what everybody tells me."

Olafson added: "We've got a pretty nice place up here, you know. Albertans tell us that all the time. Manitobans are kind of spoiled and don't always appreciate what we have."

The first four cottages are under construction. Olafson is also building a $2-million golf course. Lakefront lots sold for $55,900, golf course lots for $42,900, and backlots for $25,900. Forty remain but most are backlots.

One appeal to Albertans is that he places no time limit on when owners have to build cottages. That makes them easier for people to buy for retirement.

Many people see the Narrows eventually transforming dramatically from a sleepy sport-fishing community to a cottage and even a retirement community.

"I'd like to see it in another 50 to 100 years," said longtime resident John Johnson: "People start retiring there and next thing you know it's another Gimli."

HANDYMAN TO COTTAGE COUNTRY'S ELITE
July 19, 2004

KENORA — One thing the rich tend not to be is weekend warriors.

You aren't likely to catch them cruising hardware stores for that right part on their day off.

Nor are you likely to see them rebuilding the cottage plumbing — and cussing a blue streak when they strip the threads and have to start again.

Enter Tom Snyder, babysitter, er, property manager, to wealthy cottagers on Lake of the Woods.

"When my customers show up at the cottage, all they want to do is open the fridge and pop a beer," explained Snyder.

So Snyder does most things for them, from liquor runs, to mowing lawns, to handyman chores, to grocery shopping.

Snyder opens up cottages in spring, and closes them in fall. One year, he cleaned 326 windows on a mansion-sized cottage. (Some of the cottages he manages range from 10,000 to 12,000 square feet in size.)

Tom Snyder working at Lake of the Woods cottage

He gets the boats and motors ready, and services them again before freeze-up. And when a client hits a rock while out boating, it's Tom to the rescue. Stranded customers summon him on their cell phones.

"I take care of them, and they take very good care of me," said Snyder, 42, parent to four children ages 8 to 13. "Even for people who know the lake, it's not uncommon to hit things out there."

Not bad for someone who was without a job four years ago. Snyder left the *Winnipeg Free Press* circulation department in 2000, burned out after 19 years of trying to get newspapers out on time.

He and wife Colleen, a nurse, moved to Kenora. One day, they were at a barbecue of fairly well-to-do cottagers whom they'd never met before. The cottager asked Tom if he'd look after his place.

Soon, other cottagers were phoning him with similar requests. Today, he cares for 20 cottages, including nine year round, under T&C Property Management Services.

"What other job can you go boating or snowmobiling every other day? I look after some very big CEO cottage owners. I have people all the way from Arizona to Vancouver who have cottages on Lake of the Woods, and quite a few Winnipeggers."

He is more a jack-of-all-trades than a skilled tradesman. For more involved work, he knows the contractors and tradespeople to call.

He visits the cottages regularly to keep up their insurance coverage. And when a moth or mouse, or fallen tree, sets off a cottage's security alarm system, Snyder is summoned.

"I had to climb in a septic hole one time, after we'd cleaned it," he responds, when asked his worst job.

It takes three to four days to close a cottage for the winter. "You're talking people with four or five boats, and sprinkler systems that need to be blown out," he said. The boats he maintains range from 14 footers to a 49-foot cruiser.

In winter, cottage owners will inform him when they are coming out. Then Snyder clears the driveway and gets the heat going a couple of days in advance.

"I could probably get more business but at what point do you say I'm having a good time and doing well? Or do you say my customer is just another person in my business and you run from job to job?

"Out here, people have a different attitude. Here, they're at the lake. If you go to a job, and you want to sit around and talk for an hour, who cares?"

Social barriers tend to drop at the lake, he said. His kids sleep over at some of his customers' cottages, and his family has attended many barbecues and cocktail parties.

However, Snyder is required to sign strict confidentiality agreements with customers, agreeing not discuss who he works for, or other details. Snyder arranges parties for the cottagers, including hiring caterers and maids, and just name-dropping CEOs who attend can start business rumours.

Then there are other rumours like the one last summer that Jennifer Lopez and ex-fiancé Ben Affleck were guests at a Lake of the Woods cottage. Snyder zips his lips.

"My customers like to be here, they like to enjoy themselves, but they like to be private," he said.

The first people to build cottages at Lake of the Woods in the late 1880s tended to be rich bankers and grain barons from Winnipeg. Today, a cottage with road access sells in the $350,000 to $550,000 range; water access $250,000 to $350,000; and private island cottage from $300,000 to $700,000, said Duncan Carmichael, local real-estate broker

"We have several properties for sale in the seven figures but they're not moving quickly," Carmichael said.

There are a handful of cottage property managers in the Lake of the Woods area. Some advertise, but many simply operate privately.

The business keeps Snyder busy all summer, his days can last 12 to 14 hours. "Now I have to run to another customer whose boat lift broke," Snyder said, excusing himself.

LAKE WINNIPEG HERITAGE COTTAGES
June 14, 2009

GIMLI — John Whiteway still remembers scraping together enough loose change to buy a pack of black and white Beatle bubblegum cards back in the 1960s.

Andy Blicq's heritage cottage built in Gimli in 1918

He clanged the coins down on a store counter, opened the packs and tacked the cards to his bedroom wall at the family cottage in Gimli.

If that was at home in Winnipeg, those Beatle bubblegum cards would have been gone eons ago. Because it's the cottage, they're still up on the wall 45 years later.

Cottages seem to accumulate history like dust. Now, the province's historic resources branch has taken notice.

With some cottages approaching the century mark or more, there's a movement to change how we think about those old places. A heritage committee has started compiling an inventory of heritage cottages along the west side of Lake Winnipeg, starting with Gimli. It has also organized an open house of historic cottages in Gimli for July 11, 2009.

The province appreciates its work.

"People forget in Manitoba, cottage life is important," said David Butterfield, the province's architectural historian who co-authored with wife Maureen, *If Walls Could Talk: Manitoba's Best Buildings Explored and Explained.*

"It's a whole aspect to our recreational heritage that we would like to explore with communities like Gimli," Butterfield said.

That hasn't been the cottage way. In most parts of Manitoba, old cottages aren't called heritage buildings. They're called tear-downs. They're waiting for the owner, or the next owner, to bulldoze the joint and put up a modern 1,400-square-foot winterized home.

But that's not for everyone. Documentary filmmaker Andy Blicq, who is part of the Gimli heritage committee, is one of those who is smitten with the older cottages.

He and wife Cindy purchased their Gimli cottage in 1997 and people just assumed they would tear it down and start again. The cottage was built in 1918 and "was in pretty rough shape," Andy said.

The Blicqs had other plans. "We just loved it and wanted to restore it," he said. (It figures. Blicq was the director behind the reality series classic, *Pioneer Quest*, where two couples spent a year in the Interlake trying to survive like homesteaders did a century ago.)

So, the couple sought the advice of Leo Kristjanson, who was part of a group that restored old buildings in Gimli. (He died in 2005.) He told the Blicqs that while the cottage needed work, it was structurally sound.

That launched a 10-year restoration project. The couple stripped down and refinished the Douglas fir floor, replaced the footings, removed the plywood from the walls and buffalo board from the ceiling and the rotted windows, and replaced them with materials salvaged from other cottages being demolished. They even used material from the former fish shack at Gimli Harbour.

"There's a bit of the town everywhere in the place," said Blicq.

The result is a humble, functional and well-preserved, heritage cottage. It has an interesting, semi-circular layout.

"With Andy's cottage, there is a centre core and then you can close doors throughout, sliding doors and multiple-folding doors, and thereby close off the core in inclement weather so you have less space to warm," Butterfield said.

It's not large, by any means. The original was about 500 square feet. That included the wraparound veranda. It's larger now with the addition of indoor plumbing but not by that much.

"That's what has changed so much (with newer cottages), is the space," Blicq said. New cottages are often three times the size of the old cottages that were built with hand tools, before electricity was widely available.

Blicq dug into the history of his cottage. It was originally owned by Stefan Thorson, one of Gimli's first mayors and the father of Charlie Thorson, the illustrator credited with creating Walt Disney's Snow White and many other characters. It was built by Hjalmar (that means "builder" in Icelandic) Thorsteinson, a well-known bachelor carpenter in the area a century ago, Blicq said. A woman who once lived in the cottage used to hand out candy to children who knocked on her door and showed her good grades on their report cards.

There are other heritage lovers. The streets of Gimli are a mixture of modernized four-season homes next to small shanties, some of which look like old fishermen's shacks. It's part of the character of the community.

Margaret Goodman Wolstencroft and her husband have an eight-bedroom house in Winnipeg. Their cottage? It's 600 square feet. It was built in 1914. She's the fourth generation in her family of Goodmans to own it.

"I just can't stand changing something that means so much to our family," she said. "I thought about adding on to it, but I like it the way it is. It's what I grew up on."

The cottage was built by her great-grandfather, Carl Goodman, a Winnipeg tradesman, who constructed four Gimli cottages, all in the same design. Three are still standing.

It was built around a large, heavy oak table. That's no mistake. The table's hollowed-out pedestal was once the secret hiding place for the family's cash. "Icelanders never liked to use banks so they found other places to store their money," Wolstencroft said.

The caragana hedge around the house is also almost a century old. Inside the hedge is a low, wire fence with wooden posts. "Caragana hedges with a wire fence, that's an Icelandic thing. And the caragana never dies," she said. One theory is the wire fences were built to keep out roaming cattle.

In John Whiteway's cottage, the musty smell of the aged wood — solid Douglas fir imported from British Columbia a century ago — is very pronounced. That's because the walls, except for in the kitchen, have never been painted. The exposed wood maintains its aroma and orange patina.

The Whiteway cottage was built around 1920. He still uses an icebox manufactured in 1931.

Pots and pans hang from nails. There is an old wood stove and kerosene lanterns. (All three cottages visited had kerosene lanterns with kerosene still in them, for the nostalgia they represent and in case of power failure.) The main living area has a large linoleum square in the centre of the floor that looks like a laminated area rug.

"[The cottage] is kind of the family museum. I feel like the curator of the family museum," Whiteway said.

There are old pennants on the wall, and Icelandic Festival ribbons dating back to 1933. Like all three cottages that were visited, Whiteway's has exposed rafters. On one wall are oval portraitures of Whiteway's great-grandparents, who arrived from Devon, England, at the turn of the 20th century. Whiteway's grandfather, a railway worker, built the cottage.

Winnipeg Beach was likely the first cottage development within Manitoba. The Canadian Pacific Rail line reached there first in 1903.

Margaret Goodman's heritage cottage in Gimli

John Whiteway in his cottage built in 1920

Development at Grand Beach followed, when the Canadian Northern rail line arrived. CPR reached Gimli in 1906. Most Gimli cottages were built between the turn of the century and the 1940s.

The Gimli heritage committee has identified 33 heritage cottages in Gimli so far, and there are still more to visit. Committee chairman, Wally Johannson, a Winnipeg NDP MLA from 1969-77, hopes committee efforts will encourage other cottage communities to follow. He plans to continue making an inventory of heritage cottages for Sandy Hook, Winnipeg Beach, Whytewold and Matlock. Victoria Beach, with its vehicle ban, is another area rich in heritage cottages.

The heritage committee is also appealing to the public for help. It believes a kit or catalogue plan was used to build many of the Gimli-area cottages, likely from a lumber company. They have checked Eaton's and Aladdin kit plans but none of the building plans match those in Gimli.

"That's the missing piece of the history," Blicq said.

STONE HUTS CONTINUE TO MYSTIFY
August 5, 2007

RENNIE — First it was a mystery. Then someone came up with a reason.

Then people started shooting holes in the reason. Now it's being nudged into the mystery category again.

The mystery? Who built about 30 stone huts a century or more ago in the forests near Rennie, 130 kilometres east of Winnipeg, and why did they build them?

Lawrence Feilberg and a Rennie stone hut

Rennie resident Lawrence Feilberg came across a hut three decades ago while in the bush with his family hunting for a Christmas tree. "I thought, 'What the hell is this?'"

It was a beehive-shaped stone hut. Then he found another. And another. And many others. The largest was almost five metres in diameter. They typically stood about 1.25 metres high.

Winnipegger Walter Golke was out on a Sunday afternoon in the bush in 1988 doing some amateur prospecting "with my little hammer there to chip quartz, looking for a gold vein."

He came across a stone hut so intricately constructed that "at first I thought it was a mausoleum."

He asked around in Rennie. Many people knew about them. They loosely followed the CN rail line. Some people said Chinese railway workers slept in them, but they're really not big enough for that. Some huts are near former mining operations, giving way to speculation they were used to roast ore to extract gold.

But the most common theory he heard was they were ovens used by railroad builders a century ago.

Golke eventually surveyed and mapped out 27 of the huts in the area. He contacted Manitoba Historical Resources, which named the huts after him, although Golke says, "I no more discovered them than Columbus discovered America. Everybody in the area knew about them."

The historical branch informed him the earliest study on the huts was carried out in 1970 by University of Winnipeg anthropologist Jack Steinbring. Steinbring's study kiboshed local theory that the huts were ovens. His investigation indicated the huts may have been used to store nitroglycerin that was used for blasting through rock ridges to build the railroad. The CN rail line was built in this area in 1908.

However, CN rail had no knowledge of that. "There are actually no records because it was private contractors that built those grades for the railways," said Golke.

Provincial government archaeologists came to calling them "the Rennie Huts." Tony Buckner, an archaeologist with Historic Resources Branch at the time, published a study in 1992 in the *Manitoba Archaeological Journal.* Soil and dust samples inside huts were tested but showed no carbon to indicate ash from an oven. Neither did the stone structures match anything that pre-contact peoples had built.

What Buckner did often find was old fuel containers near the huts, supporting the theory that early railroad workers used the huts to store nitroglycerin. The huts would have stabilized air temperatures. Temperature changes could accidentally set off nitroglycerin, although according to Pierre Berton's *The Last Spike,* the real threat was cold and freezing.

Others are less sure, however. Everyone points to the large number of deaths from accidental explosions during construction of the CP Rail line. But that was 30 years earlier, and by the time CN rail's line was built, the nitroglycerin was being mixed with inert absorbents to make much safer dynamite.

Rennie resident Feilberg led the writer on a two-hour expedition through dense bush and over rock ridges to find some of the huts. It was the hottest day of the year, with the temperature nearing 37° C. Our location is kept vague to protect the huts, some of which have been vandalized.

The huts are amazingly solid and about half a dozen are still perfectly intact. "Look at the workmanship. You'd have to be a stone mason to build that," said Feilberg. It would have taken time just to find the right flat chunks of granite for materials, he said.

The huts all have entrances, and some even have lintels around the opening. "It would take two people a whole day to build one," Feilberg said.

Feilberg has more questions. Yes, the huts follow the rail line and are near tracks, but some are nearly a kilometre away. "Why would they store nitroglycerin here and walk all that way through bush and risk falling down and setting it off?" Nitroglycerin could blow up if shaken.

Some huts are on the edge of swamps. In one location, six huts line a ridge within sight of the rail line. But you would have had to go down a steep ravine, up a hill, and down another steep ravine to get there. Rail workers would definitely want to draw straws to see who carried the explosives over that terrain.

Also, why aren't the stone huts found anywhere else on the Canadian Shield? In the summer of 1908, 21,000 men were employed in railroad-building across Canada, as five railways joined forces to build what would become Canadian National Railways. One of the five, the government-owned National Transcontinental Railway, was building in this location, as part of its 2,968-kilometre line from Winnipeg to Quebec City.

But there are no other stone huts to be found. However, a larger hut in the same style, covered with dirt and used as an oven, has been discovered in Yoho National Park near Golden, B.C.

Perhaps it was a trapper who made cubbies for setting traps, said Feilberg. Or, "it could be a native thing. It's along an easy access route between lakes."

If not that, well, it could have been "some religious thing" among early peoples, he said. "I don't think this is an open and shut case at all."

THE COTTAGE COUNTRY QUESTION: TV OR NOT TV?
June 17, 2007

Whiteshell Provincial Park cottage

The annual spring ritual at our cottage isn't putting the dock in (it's not in yet because of high water), or priming the water pump (it usually involves several sprays in the face when the water pressure shoots up while you try to screw the top back on).

We don't have television at our cottage. So our annual rite is trying to find *Hockey Night in Canada* on the FM radio, 87-point-something-or-other, to listen to the playoffs.

We don't know exactly where it is on the dial. We just move the radio dial a fingernail's width at a time until we start to hear Bob Cole and Harry Neale coming in through the static, as if broadcasting from behind enemy lines. (We know Harry and Bob would do that if it meant bringing hockey games to Canada.)

But finding the signal is just half the battle. Then you have to search through the cottage for the sweet spot where the signal is loud enough that you don't have to press an ear to the speaker. While walking, you have to touch the antennae to various objects like a window, or metal table, or a loved one's anatomy. (You never know!). Some nights the signal comes through better than others.

But get satellite TV? Are you insane? We'd rather leave the door open all night for mosquitoes.

Alas, the TV-free lake experience may be going the way of outhouses and block ice. (I don't mean the second-hand TV and VCR for watching rented movies, which is quite common.) Satellite dishes are popping up on cottage rooftops like poisonous mushrooms in a wet Manitoba summer.

TV or not TV. That is the question in cottage country. It has reached the tipping point.

Cousins I know who have recently installed satellite dishes on cottages all give valid reasons. One family isn't active anymore due to age and gets tired of reading. Another set of cousins says satellite TV is the only way to get their teenage kids to the lake. I suspect people who use their cottage year-round may also feel they want TV.

Others say satellite TV isn't a big cost financially. Some companies offer six-month packages, and there's only a minimal cost if you already have a dish on your home. Then there's the most insidious of all reasons: look at how many cottages have satellite dishes already. That sounds like a tipping point reason.

I can't say we will never succumb. Yet I suspect all the promises people make to themselves to use their cottage televisions judiciously will be broken. It's a slippery slope.

Not everyone wants TV. While in the checkout line in a cottage-country store last year, I heard a woman announce to someone that she had hooked up satellite TV.

A chorus of "shame, shame" arose from people in line. TV at the lake? Sacrilege. How could you? There is still a stigma attached to having TV at the lake.

Obviously, the cottage, lake, various motor boats and toys people buy to augment the lake experience, aren't enough. What a lot of people don't know, and what a lot of cottagers won't tell you, is cottage life can be very boring.

It's a well-kept secret. Cottages are romanticized to death, but often, there's simply not enough to do.

Cottage life is often nothing more than a day broken up by small events, like going to the store, or some menial job, or reading the newspaper cover to cover. The activities are strategically spaced out to maximize their alleviation of the boredom.

But that's the thing about cottage life. You face your boredom. It seems like you have to pass through some threshold of tedium before you start to notice the birds. You stare at the lake. You start to notice plants, insects, clouds, winds, the moon, loon calls, and so on.

So before you sign on to the 100-channel universe, consider what you stand to lose.

That includes the sublime pleasure of watching your agitated wife walk through the cottage trying to find the hockey game on the radio. And the euphoria you feel when a voice emerges out of the static and it's... Don Cherry.

"That's it. Stop," I said.

My wife held up valiantly. She had the radio raised to head level because the signal would otherwise fade. She tucked her elbows in to leverage the radio, but I could see she was starting to falter.

"How long do I have to keep holding it like this?" she asked.

"Just until Coach's Corner is over," I replied.

THE MATLOCK COTTAGE THAT TIME FORGOT
July 19, 2010

MATLOCK — The joke in cottage country is that the cribbage boards are disappearing from cottages, replaced by satellite TVs.

At Augdon House, a Lake Winnipeg cottage that turned 100 years old this year, there's still a cribbage board on the mantle, and a battered old deck of playing cards not far away.

Nancy and Jim Brennan and their Matlock cottage built in 1910

There are *Time* magazines dating back to 1941 — one with German General Rommel, a.k.a. the Desert Fox, on the cover — and *Saturday Evening Posts* from the 1960s. The old magazines give the cottage a musty smell they would miss if it wasn't there, Nancy Brennan says.

And there's definitely no drywall. Everything — walls, floors, the high ceilings and the clapboard exterior — is constructed from the original timber that arrived by boat on Lake Winnipeg a century ago. "Drywall isn't a cottage," Jim Brennan says tersely.

Etiam Hic. "Still here," in Latin. That's what it says on the sign at Augdon House.

And it is still here on the southwestern shore of Lake Winnipeg, 55 kilometres north of Winnipeg.

The 2,000-square-foot, two-storey cottage looks like it can easily last another century. At the same time, it never looks like anything other than a cottage.

It still has the old slide-up, slide-down wooden windows. The walls and floors are painted boards and planks. It's not insulated.

Etiam Hic.

Indoor plumbing arrived in 1984. Before that, they used a two-hole outhouse. Owners Jim and Nancy Brennan only got a modern electric stove in 2005 because they could no longer get insurance with the old wood stove (too close to the wall).

The Brennan family is still here, too. They are big into marking history. There's a plaque on the side of the cottage put up in 1999 celebrating the 50th anniversary of the Brennan family's ownership. They've had baseball hats and other paraphernalia made out for the centennial that say, Augdon House 1910–2010. They have a guest book with the signatures of more than 2,000 names: "Everyone who's ever visited," Jim says.

There is a measuring wall recording the names and increasing heights of 28 children, grandchildren and great-grandchildren. Old black-and-white photographs of family at the cottage grace the walls and fill binders.

The cottage was built by brothers Duncan and Neil Ross, local farmers and developers who built apartment blocks on Qu'Appelle Avenue in Winnipeg. They named it the Durness House, after the coastal town in northern Scotland from which the Ross family originated.

The Ross brothers built many of the cottages at Matlock in that period. Augdon house is similar to many older cottages with its long, narrow sunroom in front. A sister of the Ross brothers even died in the cottage, with that room forever dubbed the Dead Room.

James and Florence Brennan bought the cottage in 1949. They named it Brenwick; the second syllable is after best friends the Wicketts who regularly visited. The Brennans are Irish and the next generation changed the name to Augdon House in honour of father James. Augdon is Irish and James' middle name.

Everything says cottage here, such as the Thomas Edison Amberol five-cylinder record player, manufactured in 1885, that still works. There's an ancient T. Eaton Co. shipping crate for dry goods that has served as an end table for more than half a century.

The cottage even has one of those traditional stick docks, more like a pier, that runs 120 feet into Lake Winnipeg, and 15 to 20 above the water.

It has five upstairs bedrooms and sleeps 19, including three pull-out sofas. Grandkids stay every other weekend.

The Brennans use the cottage from about May to October.

Jim, who may have a mischievous streak (he keeps a *Sarah Palin in 2012* poster in the garage "to stir things up," he said), even wrote Queen Elizabeth II, inviting her to visit Augdon House for its 100th birthday as part of her recent visit.

He didn't tell anyone and then one day Nancy called him at the office saying a letter had arrived from Buckingham Palace.

She couldn't make it, the Queen's handlers informed.